GLOBAL
COOKING

Dishes of all continents

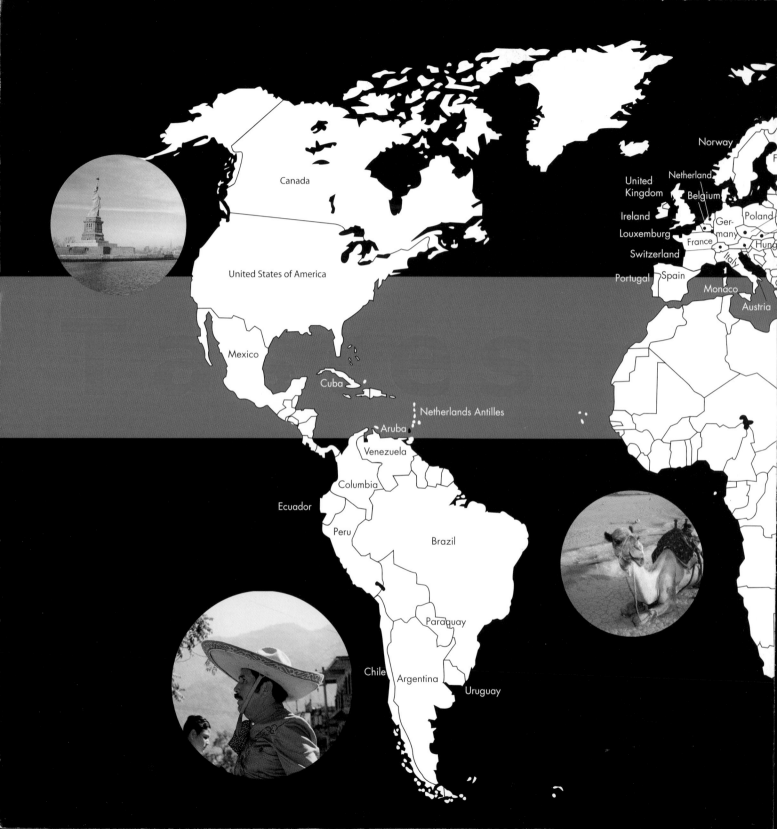

Russia

Republic
ovakia
Romania
ria
urkey

Kazakhstan

China

South-
Korea

Japan

Bahrein

India

Taiwan
Hong Kong

United
Arab
Emirates

Thai
land

Vietnam

Malaysia

Singapore

Indonesia

Mauritus

Australia

New Zealand

COLOPHON

Editor Aemily Postma
Art direction/Styling Kirsti Alink
Photography Pepijn Langedijk
Cooks Rob Beernink, Bas Hopmans
Contributors Elly de Bruin,
Sjoerd Eickmans, Susan van Heumen,
Gerard Reijmer, Anda Schippers,
Ria Tummers en Peter de Vries
Contributors photography Paul Ketelaar,
Remco Lassche, Eric van Lokven,
Picture Box, Fotostock
Translation Bothof Translation Services

© Visconti

© English edition: Miller Books 2008
email: info@miller-books.com
www.miller-books.com

ISBN 978 90 8724 056 1

FOREWORD

Global Cooking takes the reader on a culinary voyage of discovery to all the continents of the world. These dishes also give you a taste of history of the countries. If Columbus had not discovered South America, the Hungarians would not have eaten goulash with hot peppers and paprika. And if Austria had never been ruled by the mighty Hapsburgs, the cakes in the Viennese coffee houses would not have the same imperial allure. The cuisines of the world are constantly changing. Recipes and ingredients travel around the world, so that national cuisines are always open to new influences. This cookbook is full of dishes using a mixture of fantastic ingredients from countries all over the world, like freshwater fish from Luxembourg, cherries from Chile, pineapples from South Africa, crayfish from Canada, lamb from Ireland, dates from the Middle East, caviar from Russia and pecan nuts from the United States.

Global Cooking brings new dishes and methods to your familiar repertoire. With a choice of easy to prepare starters, main courses and sweets, anyone can put together international menus, organise exotic barbecues and make delightfully unusual appetisers. The anecdotes and stories behind the recipes add extra spice to an evening of international cuisine.

TABLE OF CONTENTS

Desserts

Starters and Soups

Courgette with dates and pine seeds

Kûsså ma'a tamar wa hab al-sanawbar

2 courgettes, sliced
4 tbs olive oil
30 g dried dates,
in strips
30 g pine seeds, roasted
1 clove of garlic,
chopped
pepper and salt
the juice of 1 lemon

1 Heat a frying pan and use a brush to
rub it in with olive oil.
2 Fry the slices of courgette in the pan,
in 2 or 3 portions, until they are brown.
3 Arrange the slices of courgette on
a dish.
4 Sprinkle them with chopped garlic,
the strips of dates and the roasted
pine seeds.
5 Season to taste with pepper, salt and
the lemon juice.

Lebanon

Lebanon lies on the Mediterranean coast. Nestling between Syria and Jordan, it forms the 'Fertile Crescent' where fruit, vegetables, grain, olives and legumes grow in abundance. They can be found in the mezze, the spicy starters that are renowned throughout the Middle East for their refined taste. Lebanon has made its mark on the cuisine of the Arabian world with these mezze. They are made in all sorts of varieties: pureed chickpeas, salads with sesame seed paste, dried fruit filled with cheese and a refreshing yoghurt sauce. In Lebanon, the mezze sometimes remain on the table for hours and certainly if there are guests. The numerous dishes reflect the hospitable culture of the Middle East. No one takes them away when the main course is served. But sometimes the assembled Lebanese don't even manage to eat the main course. Replete with all the savoury delicacies, the company sits and chats in a relaxed atmosphere, while enjoying a water pipe.

Spicy tuna salad

Xiang La Liang Ban Jin Qiang Yu

SPICY DICED TUNA:
350 g fresh tuna, diced
2 shallots, finely chopped
2 tbs capers
3 sprigs of coriander,
cut not too finely
the juice of ½ lemon

CURRY-VANILLA OIL:
100 ml maize oil
1 onion, chopped
1 tbs curry powder
1 vanilla pod, halved
salt and pepper

SALAD:
100 g mixed lettuce
(green and red)
2 apples, cut in strips
100 g celeriac,
diced and blanched
1 tbs balsamico vinegar
2 tbs yoghurt

GARNISH:
4 spring roll crêpes,
in triangles, deep-fried

Curry-vanilla oil (a few days in advance):
1 Fry the chopped onion in a frying pan in 2 tablespoons of oil.
2 Add a tablespoon of curry powder and allow to simmer for five minutes.
3 Heat for a few seconds with the rest of the maize oil, remove the pan from the heat, add the split vanilla pod and allow the oil to cool.

Spicy diced tuna:
1 Mix the shallots, capers, coriander, lemon juice, salt and pepper with the diced tuna.
2 Add curry-vanilla oil to taste.
3 Make a dressing for the salad with yoghurt, balsamico vinegar, salt and pepper.
4 Arrange the apple salad on each plate and add alternate layers of deep-fried crêpe triangles and the spicy tuna.
5 Sprinkle curry-vanilla oil around the dish with here and there a drop of balsamico vinegar.

Hong Kong

Apart from business, life in Hong Kong is centred on food. Eight thousand restaurants and innumerable snack outlets are a guarantee of a never-ending series of culinary surprises. The most Hong Kong Chinese originate from Guangzhou and that explains the overwhelming number of Cantonese restaurants. The taste of the Cantonese cuisine, with its emphasis on fish and seafood, is in general mild and subtle. But the peppered dishes from Szechuan are also available in Hong Kong. It is the tradition in Hong Kong to go and eat Dim Sum with the whole family on Sunday afternoons. Dim Sum is the collective name for all sorts of Cantonese snacks. In most of the larger Dim Sum restaurants the serving staff patrol the tables with trolleys containing towers of small bamboo baskets filled with the most delicious dishes. Everyone chooses from what is on offer. This manner of eating guarantees a long afternoon of enjoyment. After the first course, the time is filled with light conversation over a cup of jasmine tea, until the trolley passes once more.

Marinated salmon

Gravad laks

600 g salmon fillet, cleaned

MARINADE
70 g sea salt
50 g sugar
1 tbs black peppercorns, crushed
4 juniper berries, crushed
1 tbs mustard seed
6 twigs of dill, finely chopped

FOR THE SAUCE:
1 egg yolk, beaten
6 tbs maize oil
1 tbs sugar
1 ½ tbs vinegar
2 tbs white pepper
2 tsp salt
1 tbs mustard
2 tsp salt
2 tbs dill, finely chopped

1 Mix the ingredients for the marinade and rub it into the salmon fillet.
2 Wrap the salmon fillet tightly in plastic foil, weigh down with a plate and marinate for 24 hours in the refrigerator.
3 Rinse off the fillet and pat it dry.
4 Mix all the ingredients for the sauce.
5 Serve with the sauce, toast and a sprig of watercress.

Norway

Along the fjords at the coast and more inland on the banks of the rivers, the fishermen cast their rods in the summer to fish for salmon. In this period the fish return to their birthplace to spawn. Through fighting the current, the salmon develops strong muscles, which makes it very tasty. The patience of the Norwegian fisher folk is however tested, because wild salmon have become scarce. The last decades the fish have been grown in salmon farms in the northern fjords. The Norwegians excel in preparing this fish in tasty ways. A traditional summer dish is the Gravad laks. In the classical recipe the salmon is dressed in salt, sugar, pepper and dill and then buried in the earth for several weeks to allow the seasoning to be absorbed. Nowadays, the Norwegians preferably weigh down their salmon with plates or cans of preserved food.

Filled tacos with avocado dip

Taquitos con guacamole

FILLED TACOS:
500 g pork or chicken, diced
3 black peppercorns
1 clove of garlic, peeled
salt
1 l water
3 tbs coriander, finely chopped
1 onion, chopped
1 clove of garlic, finely chopped
3 tbs olive oil
pinch of powdered cloves
200 g tomatoes, diced
1 tbs vinegar
20 maize tortillas

GUACAMOLE:
1 shallot, finely cut
1 tomato, peeled, seeded, diced
leaves of 10 sprigs of coriander, finely chopped
1 tsp salt
1 tbs olive oil
1 green Spanish pepper
1 clove of garlic, chopped
3 ripe avocados
juice of 1 lime

Taco's:

1 Put the meat into a pan with the peppercorns, the garlic, and a pinch of salt. Add water and bring to the boil.
2 Let this simmer for 35 minutes until the meat is cooked. Allow it to cool and cut it into small pieces.
3 Heat the oil in a saucepan, add the powdered cloves and quickly fry the onion and garlic in the mixture.
4 Add the diced tomato and the meat, together with 1 tablespoon of vinegar.
5 Place a heaped tablespoonful of the mixture in the middle of each tortilla.
6 Cook the tortillas for 10 minutes in the oven at 180°C, and serve them with the guacamole.

Guacamole:

1 Puree the avocados with a fork, keep the stones.
2 Finely cut the peppers.
3 Mix the avocado puree with the other ingredients.
4 To prevent discoloration, press the stones into the puree and leave them there until the moment of serving.

Mexico

When the Spanish in the Middle Ages set foot in Mexico, they discovered that gold was not the only form of riches the country had to offer. They came in contact with, until then, unknown ingredients that up to the present day have had a major impact in kitchens in the whole world. Maize, beans, nuts, sweet potatoes, pumpkins, tomatoes, avocados, paprika, peppers and cacao, it's impossible to imagine life today without them. Typical Mexican dishes, originating from the time of the Aztecs and the Mayas, can also be found everywhere in trendy Mexican restaurants. These specialities are normally based on maize that has remained the main ingredient of every Mexican meal throughout the centuries. Maize was also very important for Indian religions. The Mayas worshipped their maize gods with long rituals and adjusted their calendars to the maize production. Maize tortillas and tacos originate from that time. They are delicious in combination with guacamole or a hot pepper sauce.

Pancakes with caviar

Blienchiki c Ikroi

1 tsp dried yeast
1 tbs sugar
150 g wheatmeal
35 g buckwheat
250 ml lukewarm milk
2 egg yolks
1 egg white
2 tbs melted butter
butter for frying
4 tbs sour cream
caviar
1 tsp salt

1 Mix the wheatmeal and buckwheat with the yeast, the sugar and 1 teaspoon of salt.
2 Add the milk and mix well, allow to rest for 15 minutes.
3 Add the egg yolks and the melted butter, beat the egg white and add it to the mixture.
4 Fry small pancakes and serve them with sour cream and caviar.

Russia

Russia's most well-known culinary treat is caviar, the roe of the sturgeon. The eighteenth century Russian nobility flaunted this delicacy on their sakuska, the buffet for starters. The person's status could be determined by the number of kilos of fish eggs. Caviar is still a symbol of luxury and prosperity in Russia. Therefore, the majority of Russians only enjoy this delicacy during a festive dinner. But for centuries the fishermen of the Caspian Sea ate it as a main dish together with potatoes boiled in their jackets. Caviar on a butter blini, the Russian pancake, with a nut of sour cream, forms a delicious combination. A blini is also compared to a little sun and is a symbol of rich harvests and happy marriages. It is a desired dish, especially during the week before lent, the butter week. This is followed by forty days of sobriety and penitence, after which the well to do Russians can carefully risk caviar again, on white bread with butter.

Lamb meatballs with ouzo and tzatziki

Keftedákia me ouzo & tzatziki

FOR THE MINCE:
3 slices of stale bread
(white or brown)
1 large onion, grated
500 g minced lamb
5 tbs parsley,
finely chopped
1 clove of garlic,
finely chopped
1 small egg, beaten
2 tbs ouzo
¼ tsp cinnamon
salt, freshly ground pepper

TO FRY:
app. 50 g flour
app. 125 ml (Greek) olive
oil

TZATZIKI:
1 large cucumber
2 dl yoghurt, drained or
Greek yoghurt
⅛ l sour cream or crème
fraîche
2-3 cloves of garlic,
finely chopped or crushed
1 tbs olive oil
salt, pepper, pinch of sugar
app. ¾ tbs wine vinegar
2 tbs freshly chopped
mint or dill

1 Mix all of the ingredients for the mince well.
2 Make app. 25 balls from the mix and roll them in the flour.
3 Heat the oil in a large anti-stick frying pan and brown and cook the mince balls on a high flame.
4 Allow them to drain on kitchen towel and serve them hot.

Tzatziki:
1 Grate the washed and peeled cucumber with a coarse grater or cut them into fine strips. Allow them to drain or press out as much moisture as possible in a clean tea towel.
2 Beat the yoghurt, together with the sour cream, into a creamy mix and stir in the garlic, cucumber, oil and some salt, pepper and sugar.
3 Add vinegar and if desired some fresh herbs. Serve tzatziki well cooled.

Greece

In Greece eating mainly means being in good company and preferably away from home. The Greeks are known for the fact that they will make even a normal weekday special by having a few drinks with friends on the terrace of a taverna or ouzerie. There they order mezethes, hot and cold snacks, which are similar to the mezze from the Middle East. The origin of these dishes is not really clear. In any case they spread because of shifting power bases, emigration and trade missions. In Greece they are absolutely at home. They are an excellent complement to ouzo, the best known Greek apéritif. The slightly sweet aroma of this drink requires snacks with contrasting and explicit tastes, such as salted sardines, black olives, strong types of cheese, spiced meatballs from lamb and tzatziki. For those who would like to do something other than barbecue with friends or family on a sultry summer evening, mezethes offer a surprising alternative.

Potato soup with mushrooms

Sumavask bramborov polèvka

40 g butter
100 g mushrooms, sliced
50 g cream
300 g potatoes, diced
4 eggs
1 l beef bouillon
1 tbs lemon juice
salt, pepper, vinegar,
bay lea

1 Fry the mushrooms in the butter.
2 Boil the diced potatoes in the bouillon,
  with the bay leaf and a dash of
  vinegar.
3 Remove the bay leaf and blend the
  potato and bouillon with a hand
  blender or in a food processor into
  a smooth soup.
4 Add to this the mushrooms and cream.
5 Add salt, pepper and lemon juice
  to taste.
6 Beat one egg into each soup bowl and
  pour the soup on top of it.

Czech Republic

The Czech Republic, in the heart of Europe, hides a treasury of historic monuments. The rich culture is gathered together especially in Prague. In the old city, stare mesto, various styles can be seen. After a day strolling around the streets of this part of the city, visitors can visit the new city, nove mesto, for their evening activities. This can start with a fantastic dinner in one of the romantic restaurants, followed by an opera or a ballet. A nightcap in one of Prague's beer cellars is certainly to be recommended to round off the evening. After a visit to Prague it is pleasant to travel around the countryside, for instance in the Sumava district, where the Czech composer Smetana allowed himself to be inspired by the presence of the Moldau River. A soup that is eaten throughout the Czech Republic can be found on the menu here with fresh wild mushrooms from the surrounding forests. This dish will remind whoever has visited Sumava of the mountains, forests and the Moldau.

Nem spring rolls

Nem Cuon Song

100 g lean pork
60 g thin Chinese noodles
125 g small shrimps
75 g bean sprouts
3 tbs ground peanuts
2 tbs coriander leaves, chopped
12 sheets of rice paper (bánh trang)

TO SERVE WITH IT:
fresh lettuce
coriander leaves

FOR THE PHUANG NAM DIP SAUCE:
2 tbs fish sauce
2 tbs rice vinegar or white wine vinegar
1 tbs water
1 tsp ginger, very finely chopped
1 tsp sugar
2 small, fresh, red or green Spanish peppers, finely chopped
1 clove of garlic, finely chopped

1 Mix all of the ingredients for the dip sauce and divide it up into bowls for each person.
2 Cook the pork in a pan of water until it is just cooked.
3 Allow it to drain and then chop it up very finely. Put it aside.
4 Boil a saucepan full of clean water.
5 Put the Chinese noodles in a long-handled wire basket and plunge them in the boiling water for 10 seconds.
6 Then plunge them immediately in cold water to halt the cooking process.
7 Allow the noodles to drain, break them in large pieces and put them aside.
8 Blanch the shrimps in the same way, for a maximum of 5 seconds. Allow them to drain, then chop them up very finely and put them aside.
9 Blanch the bean sprouts as well, for approximately 10 seconds.
10 Give each guest a plate containing a folded napkin that has been drenched in cold water.
11 Arrange the blanched ingredients together on a plate with the rice paper and the mounds of peanuts and coriander.
12 Put this on the table with the bowls of dip sauce and a separate plate containing the lettuce and mint.
13 Make spring rolls by moistening the rice paper with the damp napkins.
14 Then place a row of blanched ingredients on each sheet of rice paper.
15 Sprinkle the filling with peanuts and coriander.
16 Fold one edge of the rice paper over the filling and role it carefully up into a pipe; the moistened paper will adhere to itself so that the spring roll will remain closed.
17 Dip the spring rolls in the sauce and eat them together with the lettuce and the leaves of mint.

Vietnam

Whoever is invited to a meal with a Vietnamese family will be surprised by the spectacle of rituals. It is worth the effort to arrive early, when the preparations are still in full swing. The visitor will often find the host or hostess sitting cross-legged on the kitchen floor. The dishes are stirred using bamboo spatulas in a wok above the open fire. Not much later the family will gather around a low table with a steaming bowl of rice, a pan of soup, a dish of green vegetables and a plate full of spring rolls. The aroma of spices stimulates the nostrils. The herbs are almost always used fresh, so that the taste comes to the fore. Around the Vietnamese New Year, life is centred more or less completely around the kitchen. In this period a special ceremony is dedicated to the god of the kitchen, Tao Quan. There is a chance that he might inspire anyone who wants to make his or her own spring rolls.

Pitta bread with mince & bean caviar

Arepas rellenas con guiso de carne & Caviar Criollo

PITTA BREAD WITH MINCE:
2 tbs olive oil
250 g minced beef
250 g minced pork
1 onion, cut in 2
4 green peppers,
diced, seeded
400 g peeled tomatoes,
diced
½ tsp powdered cumin
1 sprig of thyme,
(only the leaves)
pepper and salt
12 olives filled with
pimento, diced
1 tbs capers
8 pitta bread, toasted

BEAN CAVIAR:
225 g black beans,
cooked
2 tbs olive oil
1 shallot, finely cut
1 red pepper, seeded,
finely chopped
3 cloves of garlic,
finely chopped
pinch of cumin powder
salt

1 Heat the oil in a heavy casserole over a medium flame.
2 Add the mince, onion, garlic, chilli pepper, tomatoes and herbs.
3 Cook for 20 minutes stirring occasionally, until the tomatoes have formed a thick sauce.
4 Stir in the olives and capers.
5 Fill the pitta bread with the mixture and serve them warm with bean caviar.

Bean caviar:
1 Fry the shallot with the pepper and garlic for 2 minutes in the olive oil.
2 Mix in the beans and puree the mixture with a hand blender or in a food processor.

Venezuela

Venezuela is one of the largest oil exporting countries in the world. Before oil was found, it was one of the poorest countries of South America. Since the arrival of the oil industry in the nineteen twenties, there has been a rapid increase in prosperity. The country lies on the north coast of South America, close to the Caribbean Sea. Venezuelans originate from Europeans, indians and Africans, which has allowed a mixture of eating habits to arise. Apart from fish dishes, black beans, cooking bananas and rice are very popular. These dishes are mainly eaten in combination with arepas, a type of soft tortilla pancake. Caviar Cirollo, which goes extremely well with arepas, is actually a type of Spanish tapenade, based on the Venezuelan black bean.

Creamy avocado soup with potatoes

Sopa de aguacate y papas

3 leeks, the white part, thinly cut
2 medium size potatoes, peeled and thinly cut
1 l poultry stock
200 ml sour cream
salt and pepper to taste
1 avocado, pureed

GARNISH:
sour cream
2 tomatoes, peeled, seeded, diced
coriander leaves
red pepper, in thin strips
1 avocado, diced

1 Bring the stock to boil and add the leek and potatoes.
2 Allow this to simmer for approximately 20 minutes until the vegetables are soft.
3 Puree the soup with a hand blender.

Serving:
1 Mix the avocado puree with the sour cream.
2 Stir this mixture into the soup just before serving, heating for too long makes the avocado bitter.
3 Garnish the avocado soup with the diced tomato and avocado, coriander leaves, strips of red pepper and cream.
4 Serve hot or cold.

Colombia

Soup plays an important role in the Colombian kitchen. A comida – meal – without soup is more or less unheard of. The soups are rich and varied. They combine ingredients from the Old and the New Worlds, as South America was called after Columbus discovered it. They are often full-bodied soups with fresh vegetables, chicken or beef, pasta or rice, cheese, cream and eggs. Although the avocado is an authentic South American product that has been used in salads and sauces for centuries, avocado soup is a relative new comer. The Colombian variant is made with potatoes from the Andes.

Canadian crayfish salad

Salade de homard canadien

2 crayfish of 400 g each,
alive
1 head of cabbage lettuce
8 quail eggs
10 radishes
12 blades of chives

FOR THE SAUCE:
1 egg yolk
150 ml maize oil
Tabasco
1 tbs lemon juice
salt
½ tbs Dijon mustard
1 tbs ketchup
1 tbs whisky

1 Bring 4 litres of water to the boil with 2 tablespoons of sea salt, put in the crayfish and keep the water almost boiling. The crayfish is cooked in approximately 5 minutes. Allow the crayfish to cool in the liquor.
2 Hard boil (5 minutes) the quail eggs and remove the shells.
3 Slice the radishes.
4 Mix the egg yolk with mustard, lemon juice and salt.
5 Add the oil in a thin stream while beating the mixture. Continue to beat until a thick sauce is created, flavour with ketchup and whisky.
6 Cut the crayfish in two and clean them.
7 Serve the flesh of the crayfish with the sauce and the slices of radish on a bed of cabbage lettuce.

Canada

Canadian cuisine reflects the origins of its inhabitants. French, English, Scots, Irish, Germans, Poles, Ukrainians, Scandinavians and Icelanders have introduced their own dishes. This has resulted in a mixed culinary culture, where the use of Canadian ingredients forms the common thread – fish, crustaceans and shellfish, maize, rice, game, poultry, berries and fungi. The Canadian fusion cooking has developed to a high level, especially in the province of Ontario. In the restaurants there is an enormous variety of innovative and experimental dishes available. However, freshwater fish and crayfish, from the many lakes and rivers in this area, normally remain the favourites of the Canadian cook.

Risotto ai carciofi

300 g risotto rice
2 artichokes
60 g shallot, diced
1 clove of garlic, chopped
1 lemon, squeezed
out in water
1 tbs olive oil
600 ml chicken or
vegetable stock
50 g butter
50 g parmesan cheese,
grated
pepper and salt

FOR THE GARNISH:
1 à 2 artichokes
Parmesan cheese
basil or sage leaves
olive oil

1 Wash the artichokes and cut of the stalks so that only 4 cm remains.
2 Break off the leaves just above the fleshy hearts and remove the fibres. Dunk the artichokes in the lemon water.
3 Clean the hearts and cut them into cubes of 3 x 3 mm.
4 Fry them together with the garlic and the diced shallot in oil, but don't let then turn brown.
5 Add the rice and fry for 2-3 minutes.
6 Add the stock little by little. Ensure that the stock is wholly absorbed before more is added. Continue in this manner until the rice has reached the required readiness.
7 Flavour the risotto with the butter, parmesan cheese, pepper and salt.

Garnish:
1 Clean the artichokes and cut the hearts into 2 mm thick slices.
2 Deep-fry the slices until they are crisp in olive oil at 170°C, and then sprinkle them with salt.
3 Deep-fry the sage leaves until they are crisp in olive oil at 170°C, and sprinkle them with salt.

Italy

Italy has a very diverse landscape and a great variety of farming produce. Therefore, every area has its own dishes that are based on the ingredients from the region. The local differences can also be found in the cooking of North and South Italy. In the south, dishes are in the main prepared with olive oil; in the north often with butter and cream. The southern part of Italy is mainly famous for its variety of pastas, while risotto is a typical dish from Northern Italy. But a basic dish such as risotto with artichoke is known throughout the whole Mediterranean region. Despite the many regional differences, the Italians have a common culinary tradition. The whole Italian cuisine is characterised by authenticity, simplicity, variety and high-quality supply. Although life it is increasingly busy in the cities, Italians still take time out to enjoy their food. To be able to do this is still, just as in the past, considered to be an art of living.

Ravioli with yoghurt and mint

Manti

FOR THE DOUGH:
400 g flour from durum
1 tsp salt
4 tbs oil
2 eggs
80 ml water

FOR THE FILLING:
500 g minced mutton
1 tbs olive oil
1 tsp salt
1 tsp black pepper
2 shallots, chopped

FOR THE SAUCE:
60 ml olive oil
4 cloves of garlic,
finely chopped
200 ml yoghurt
2 tomatoes, peeled,
seeded, diced
salt
1 red hot pepper, chopped
1 tbs mint

1 Mix the ingredients for the dough and knead them into a stiff dough.
2 Cover with foil and allow to rest for app. 30 minutes.
3 Sauté the shallot in 1 tablespoonful of olive oil, add the mince, fry until cooked and flavour it to taste.
4 Roll out the dough using a long thin stick (an 'oklava', or Turkish pasta rolling pin). Roll it as thin as possible. Cut it into squares. Put a teaspoon full of filling onto each square and fold them shut.
5 Cook the filled squares.
6 Mix the yoghurt with the olive oil, tomato, mint and pepper, serve this sauce off-warm with the pasta.

Turkey

The nomads laid the foundations for the rich Turkish cuisine, centuries ago. At the time of the Ottoman empire, palace cooks further perfected Turkish cooking. They refined the Turkish dishes to gain their sultans' favour and to ensure the status of these leaders. The abundance of natural food sources has had an influence on Turkish cooking. But the social importance that the Turks attach to food played just as important a role in the culinary developments. In Turkey, food stands for being together with family and friends and is a symbol of hospitality. Manti is a popular Turkish dish that originated in the times of the nomads. It will rarely be missing from a typical Turkish picnic. Sitting on a carpet, the whole family eats from a single plate. After which it is great to relax in the shadows while the most musical member of the family sings a nostalgic song and plays the saz.

Salade Monégasque

500 g tomatoes,
seeded, in quarters
3 red peppers,
seeded, in strips
1 red onion, in small rings
2 artichoke hearts,
raw, thinly cut
200 g broad beans,
cleaned
200 g tuna in oil
50 g black olives
1 cucumber, peeled,
seeded, in slices
4 tbs olive oil
2 tbs lemon juice
salt
basil leaves

1 Mix all the vegetables in a bowl, add olive oil, lemon juice, pepper and salt.
2 Distribute the tuna in large chunks over the top.
3 Add the olives.
4 At the last moment flavour the salad with basil leaves.

Monaco

Monaco is the country of the Grand Prix, of the casino and the luxurious yacht harbour of the capital Monte Carlo. The small principality on the Mediterranean has an enormous attraction for prosperous business people and well-known artists, who take pleasure in placing a bet, attending cocktail parties or worshipping the Mediterranean sun. In the evening impeccably dressed waiters serve martinis and champagne to film stars on Monte Carlo's boulevard terraces. Here people also enjoy countless refined snacks, before proceeding on to one of the comfortable restaurants. Salad Monégasque can often be found as a starter on the menu. This delicacy is an equivalent of the well-known Niçoise salad.

Potato salad with walnuts, cheese and chilli sauce

Papa Huancaina

4 potatoes, in their jackets, washed

FOR THE SAUCE:
100 ml peanut oil
50 ml milk
1 onion, finely chopped
2 cloves of garlic, chopped
4 red Spanish peppers, seeded, finely cut
150 g fresh cheese
pepper and salt

FOR THE GARNISH:
1 head of lettuce, washed, without the outer leaves
4 hard-boiled eggs, cut in parts
12 black olives, stoned
½ red paprika, cut in thin strips
100 g walnuts

1 Cook the potatoes in their jackets and let them cool.
2 Heat the oil in a thick-bottomed saucepan and sauté the onion, garlic and Spanish peppers on a low heat until the onion is soft.
3 Stir in the cheese and the milk and put the sauce in a food processor or blender.
4 Puree the mass until a smooth sauce is obtained that has the consistency of mayonnaise, flavour the sauce with pepper and salt

Presentation:
1 Cover a large plate with lettuce leaves.
2 Peel the potatoes, cut them into thick slices and place them in overlapping rows over the lettuce.
3 Pour the sauce over the top and garnish the dish with pieces of egg, olives, walnuts and strips of paprika.

Peru

The history of the potato lies high in the Peruvian Andes where this root originally came from. It was cultivated first by the Incas who attached great importance to it. The potato was not only a food but also a medicine, a poison and an ingredient used by witches. Apart from the root, the Incas extracted the bitter juice from the stems. They used this to preserve peppers, meat, fruits and vegetables. A poisonous substance extracted from the fruit of the plant was used as an insecticide. And they made women's hair decorations from the flowers, which occur in all colours of the rainbow. Children, who were born in June when the crop was harvested, were called 'brother or sister of the potato'. There are many different potato dishes in Peru. The most popular is the papa Huancaina, which is pre-pared slightly differently in each region.

Gazpacho

1000 g tomatoes in tomato juice
2 cucumbers
1 red paprika
1 onion, cleaned, chopped
1 red Spanish pepper, seeded
salt and pepper
1 clove of garlic, peeled
2 tbs sherry vinegar
4 tbs olive oil
fresh parsley or coriander
white bread

1 Peel and cut 1 ½ cucumber, ½ a paprika and the tomatoes into large pieces.
2 Blend these together with the onion, garlic and the pepper in a blender and then pass the mixture through a sieve.
3 Flavour the soup with salt, pepper, olive oil and sherry vinegar and leave in the refrigerator until very cold.
4 Dice the rest of the vegetables and serve them in separate dishes with the soup, together with cubes of white bread.
5 To cool the soup even further, just prior to serving add some crushed ice.

Spain

All of the characteristics that make Spain what it is can be found in the southern region of Andalusia. In cities such as Granada and Seville, the domes of mosques and the towers of cathedrals stand out against the clear blue sky. Whitewashed houses with inviting inner courtyards cluster around picturesque squares. These are often the setting for fiestas where the passionate sounds from the flamenco guitar ring out over the rooftops. In the countryside, acres of olive trees alternate with immense fields of tomatoes. And in the wine growing area of Jerez de la Frontera there are the sherry bodegas with the oak casks piled high. Andalusia is also the place of origin of Spain's most well-known dish: the gazpacho, a refreshing cold vegetable soup. In the sweltering heat of the Andalusian summer, this culinary masterpiece is a great thirst quencher.

Trout in riesling

F'rel am Reisleck

2 trout
200 ml riesling
150 ml cream
50 ml fish stock
2 tbs salted butter
4 tbs of mixed parsley,
tarragon, chervil and chive
2 shallots, finely chopped
pepper and salt

1 Lightly fry the trout for 2 to 3 minutes on both sides in 1 tablespoon of butter.
2 In the meantime, butter an oven dish, and when ready place the trout in it.
3 Sauté the shallot and add the riesling, cream and stock.
4 Bring this sauce to the boil, add it to the trout, cover the dish and put it in an oven at 180°C for 15 minutes.
5 Remove the trout, fillet them and divide the fillets over the four plates.
6 Sieve the sauce and reduce it on the heat to the desired thickness while beating all the time.
7 Serve the trout together with the herbs.

Luxembourg

The specialities of Luxembourg have their origin in the robust and strong cooking of the countryside. But the country has in the main developed its culinary dishes under the influence of its German and French neighbours. The well forested north of Luxembourg, that forms part of the Ardennes, is well-known for its delicious game. In the undulating country of the south, where there are many river valleys, fish dishes can be enjoyed. The country produces wonderful wines, such as the rieslings from the area around the banks of the Moselle. These form a perfect combination with river fish. Apart from being served in the glass, riesling is often used in cooking. How surprising that can be is shown by this recipe for trout in riesling sauce.

Shrimp cocktail

Cheviche de Camerón

20 peeled shrimp, number 5
3 tomatoes, halved
1 onion, cleaned, halved
2 jalapeño peppers or Spanish peppers (these are somewhat milder)
1 red paprika
2 tbs lime juice
4 tbs orange juice
salt
hot pepper sauce to taste

GARNISH:
2 tbs red onion, finely chopped
1 tbs chives, cut
1 tbs coriander leaf or parsley
2 tbs popcorn
2 tbs grains of maize

1 Bring to the boil 1 litre water with 1 table-spoon of salt, add the shrimps for 30 seconds.
2 Allow the shrimps to cool and drain on a piece of kitchen towel on a plate.
3 Grill the tomatoes, peppers, paprika and onion for 6 to 8 minutes on a hot plate in the oven or in a frying pan.
4 Put the grilled vegetables on a tray and cover them with foil, allow them to rest for 15 minutes.
5 Mix the lemon and orange juice in a blender, then strain it.
6 Marinate the shrimps in the juice for at least 1 hour.
7 Before serving, mix in the red onion, coriander, popcorn and grains of maize.

Ecuador

Ecuador is a country of large expanses of wonderful, virgin nature. The Andes extend through the heart of the country, while the east is dominated by the sweltering Amazon area. In the western low lands banana and cacao plantations extend to the long palm-fringed beaches of the coast. From there travellers can take the boat to the breathtaking Galapagos islands. They are a favourite place for walkers, people looking for a rest and divers. The restaurants on the coast of Ecuador are renowned for their cheviche, a fish dish with shrimps that are marinated in lemon juice. It is like the raditional European shrimp cocktail, were it not for the fact that this starter has made an exotic detour.

Main Courses

Hearty noodle soup with coconut milk, shrimps and chicken

Laksa lemak

6 sprigs daun salaam
2 cm root ginger, finely chopped
1 litre water
150 ml thick coconut milk
1 tbs sugar
500 g thin fresh yellow mee (or dried mee, cooked and drained)
150 g bean sprouts, blanched
1 chicken breast, steamed, cut into pieces
100 g peeled shrimps, steamed
salt

SPICE PASTE:
4 tbs groundnut oil
8 red chilli peppers
10 shallots
1 stalk lemon grass
½ tsp dried shrimp paste

GARNISH:
1 tbs root ginger, sliced
1 cucumber, cut into pieces
3 eggs, made into an omelette and cut into strips
2 red chilli peppers, chopped
2 spring onions, finely chopped
6 small, round limes
6 tbs sambal

1 Finely chop and grind the ingredients for the spice paste.
2 Add a little oil if necessary to make the paste easier to grind.
3 Heat the remaining oil and fry the ground ingredients on a low heat for 10 minutes, stirring occasionally.
4 Add the daun salaam, ginger and water and bring to the boil.
5 Add the coconut milk, sugar and salt.
6 Lower the heat and simmer gently, uncovered, for 10-15 minutes.
7 Place the mee in boiling water for a few seconds.
8 Divide the mee, chicken, bean sprouts and shrimps into 6 small bowls.
9 Add the paste and garnish with a little cucumber, omelette, chillies and spring onions.
10 Serve with the belacan sambal and limes pieces on a separate plate.

Tip: The paste can be prepared in advance. The ingredients for the garnish can be assembled in advance, but should only be chopped just before serving to retain maximum taste and aroma. If you cannot get fresh mee, you can use dried rice vermicelli or any other dried Chinese wheat noodles.

Malaysia

Malaysia is a large peninsula on the southern tip of the Asian continent. This cultural crossroads has for centuries been a port of call for trading fleets from the Middle East, India and Europe. The Javanese and Chinese have also left their mark. The largest population group in Malaysia is descended from the original Chinese who settled there 4,000 years ago. Later, under British rule, there was a further influx of Indian and Chinese workers. This stream of immigrants exerted a strong influence on the local cuisine. Cultural interaction has given rise to unique Malaysian dishes. These can be recognised primarily in the varied and exotic Nonya cuisine, which combines hot and spicy foods with subtlety and simplicity. Many dishes are bathed in a mild, creamy coconut sauce, like this spicy mee soup from the Nonya cuisine of Malacca.

Stewed fish with horseradish sauce

Ryba w sosie chrzanowym

2 carrots
1 stick celery
1 cm horseradish
1 onion, cut into quarters
5 peppercorns
1 bay leaf
2 tsp salt
1.5 litres water
1 kg fish fillets

FOR THE SAUCE:
3 tbs butter
3 tsp flour
3 tbs grated horseradish
1 tsp sugar
¼ tsp salt
150 ml sour cream
2 hard-boiled eggs,
peeled and finely chopped

1 Mix the vegetables, herbs and water in a pan and bring to the boil. Simmer for 20 minutes, then strain off the stock.
2 Boil the fish for 6 to 10 minutes in the stock.
3 Melt butter in the pan, mix with the flour to form a roux.
4 Add 200 ml stock and cook, stirring continuously, until you have a smooth sauce.
5 Remove from heat and mix sauce with the egg, sour cream and horseradish.
6 Season with salt and sugar and serve.

Poland

In Poland, many meals are prepared for festive occasions, like the traditional Christmas Eve meal, Wigilia. The menu on Christmas Eve consists of twelve courses, representing the twelve apostles. Some families serve thirteen to include Christ. The meal begins when the first star appears in the sky: a metaphor for the star of Bethlehem. Since the period of fasting does not end until midnight, the Christmas meal does not include meat. But this makes it no less delicious or festive. There are no strict rules about standard dishes in this Christmas menu. The choice varies according to region, and depends on the ingredients available. Special rituals are observed in serving the meal. Some families represent the crib by laying straw under the tablecloth. Often an extra place is laid for the uninvited guest. This fish in horseradish sauce is usually the first course on the Wigilia menu.

Lamb with exotic herbs

Al-Tashriba ma'a Baharat

4 aubergines
150 g chick peas, soaked
500 g lamb or mutton,
cut into 3 cm pieces
4 tbs oil
1 onion, finely chopped
200 ml sieved tomatoes
salt
1 tbs lemon juice
2 pitta breads

BAHARAT SPICE MIXTURE:
1 tbs black peppercorns
1 tsp coriander seed
½ tsp cumin seed
6 cardamom pods
1 cinnamon stick
pinch of ground nutmeg
1 cm root ginger, chopped
1 tbs paprika

1 Wash the aubergines, cut them in pieces and fry in 2 tbs oil.
2 Brown the meat in 2 tbs oil and remove from pan.
3 Put the shredded onion in the pan and sauté till tender.
4 Add the tomato sauce and cook for 10 minutes.
5 Return the meat to the pan, together with the chick peas.
6 Add salt and the baharat spice mixture (see below), and a little water if required, until the meat is almost submerged.
7 Cook, covered, over a low heat until the meat and chick peas are tender.
8 Serve with pitta breads

Baharat spice mixture:
1 Roast the spices in a hot dry pan until browned (not blackened!).
2 Grind to a powder and mix with the paprika.
3 Put the baharat in a sealed container and store in a cool place.

Bahrein

Bahrein, a group of islands in the Persian Gulf, is an important financial centre and is a favourite holiday destination for people from the surrounding countries. This gulf state is also an international conference centre. No wonder that Bahrein has some of the best foreign restaurants, offering Japanese sushi, Italian pasta and Indian curries. Of course Arab dishes are also served. They are characterised by the exotic aroma of baharat, a mixture of spices for the preparation of lamb and beef dishes. Baharat consists of spices introduced thousands of years ago through trade with the Far East, dates and incense being exchanged for coriander, cinnamon and cardamom. As well as baharat, the meat dishes of the Gulf often contain rose water or orange blossom water. This practice dates from the Middle Ages. However modern Bahrein may be in many respects, its meat dishes bring centuries of history to the table.

Potato dumplings with sheep's cheese

Bryndzove halusky

1 kg peeled potatoes,
grated
400 g flour
300 g sheep's cheese or
cottage cheese
200 g bacon
salt
1 tbs chopped chives

1 Mix the flour with the potato and salt to form a dough. Form this into small balls and drop them into boiling, salted water.
2 Boil the dumplings for about 10 minutes until they are tender and rise to the surface. Cut the bacon into thin strips and fry in a frying pan.
3 Drain the dumplings and transfer them to a dish. Cover with sheep's cheese (or cottage cheese), bacon and chives. The potato dumplings can also be prepared with sour cream, butter and dill.

Slovakia

Anyone touring in the Slovakian mountains has to make frequent stops to let large flocks of sheep cross the road. Traditional cheesemakers still use their milk to make sheep's milk quark: the typically Slovakian bryndza. The milk is first strained through cloth, then the smooth, moist mixture is dried for a week. This short fermentation gives the bryndza its characteristic sour taste. To improve the keeping qualities of the sheep's cheese, it is often hung up to smoke in special smoking chambers. Bryndza forms the basis of strapacky and halusky, two traditional Slovakian dishes. This bryndza distinguishes the Slovakian from the Czech cuisine. Noodles and other starchy foods are very popular in both countries. In Slovakia the noodles are often accompanied by sheep's milk quark. While the Czechs are real beer drinkers, Slovaks prefer a good glass of wine, preferably home-grown. And wine is the best accompaniment for these potato dumplings with sheep's cheese.

Aubergine salad with pimiento dressing

Ensalade de beranjenas con salsa de pimientos

250 g aubergines, diced
1 clove garlic, crushed
1 tbs lime or lemon juice
salt
1 spring onion,
finely chopped
1 stick of celery,
finely chopped
a few lettuce leaves

DRESSING:
100 g red peppers
(pimientos)
1 tbs white vinegar
1 tsp mustard
60 ml buttermilk or milk

1 Place the diced aubergines in a little water and bring to the boil.
2 Add the garlic, lime or lemon juice and some salt and cook the aubergines for 10 minutes until just tender.
3 Strain aubergines and leave to cool.
4 In the meantime prepare a dressing by combining all the dressing ingredients in a food processor.
5 If necessary add a little more buttermilk or milk until you have a creamy dressing.
6 Mix the cooled aubergines with the spring onion and celery and season the vegetables with salt to taste.
7 Pour dressing over the aubergine mixture and serve immediately.
8 Serve with rice and beans.

Uruguay

In Uruguay as in the rest of South America, the pepper is a very popular and much-used food. It is probably one of the greatest treasures of the 'New World'. According to experts, peppers were first cultivated in the Valley of Mexico in 7000 BC. Since they were first exported in colonial times they have spread like wildfire throughout the world. There are estimated to be at least hundred varieties of pepper, each with a different taste, shape and colour. The pimiento is a sweet red pepper, which, outside South America, is particularly popular in Hungary and Spain. There are six types of pimiento, on a scale from mild to hot. In Uruguay it is eaten as hot as possible with aubergines. Perhaps these ingredients go so well together because they originate from the same family.

Lamb with rice

Pilav

600 g mutton,
in long strips
1 tbs butter
3 shallots, cut into rings
6 bunched carrots, in strips
300 g pilau rice
1 litre water or
poultry stock
100 g dried apricots
or apples
salt and pepper to taste

1 Brown the meat well in a casserole dish.
2 Add the shallot rings and carrot strips,
  and fry for a further 3 minutes or so.
3 Add the rice and then a little later
  the stock.
4 Cover this with dried apricots or apples.
5 Cover the dish and leave to cook slowly
  for about 90 minutes.

Kazakhstan

The population of Kazakhstan was reliant for centuries on herds of sheep, camels and horses. These were their guarantee of transport, clothing and food. These nomadic tribes had a strong family hierarchy, which extended to the distribution of food. Of the stewed lamb which formed the main constituent of a meal, the leg was given to the older people, as a token of respect. The brisket went to the sons and daughters-in-law and the other pieces were shared among the rest of the tribe. The sheep's head went to the guest of honour. Even nowadays the Kazakhs are real meat eaters, but their cooking has developed continuously under the influence of Russians, Uzbecks, Tartars, and Koreans. Their diet would now be in-conceivable without vegetables, fruit and cereals. Kazakhstani pilav is served at weddings on oval serving dishes. The dish looks very festive with its long strips of carrot. The apricots give this rice dish an exotic flavour.

Chicken San Pei

San Bei Ji

3 chicken legs or four
medium-sized squid
2 cm root ginger,
finely chopped
8 cloves garlic,
finely chopped
1 tbs red chilli,
finely chopped
12 basil leaves
50 ml white wine
2 tbs dark sesame oil
4 tbs light soy sauce
1 tbs palm sugar

1 Cut the chicken legs into four or five
   pieces (or cut the squid into rings).
2 Put a wok or casserole on a high heat.
3 Add the dark sesame oil and the ginger
   and wait until the aroma develops.
4 Add the garlic, chilli, soy sauce,
   wine, sugar and the chicken (or squid).
5 Stir well and bring to the boil.
6 Turn down the heat and simmer,
   covered, for 20 minutes.
7 Add the basil leaves and wait
   30 seconds.
8 Serve on a serving dish.

Taiwan

A magnificent mountainous landscape, volcanic coastline and waterfalls in the mist make Taiwan an idyllic island. But the beauty and serene calm of the countryside cannot be found in the capital, Tai Pei. Here visitors are deluged by the hectic round-the-clock bustle of business. The same applies to the food trade in the lively night markets. As in the rest of the country, it is predominantly Chinese food which is served in the many small cafes. But Taiwanese cooking is different from Chinese in that it uses more sugar, has a subtropical aroma and shows a predilection for fish. Oyster omelettes, squid bouillon and noodles are favourite snacks. Kip San Pei is a popular meat dish, which can be made with squid instead of chicken. After this spicy dish you need something to quench your thirst. In Taiwan this is simply a matter of choosing between competing fruit juice, ice cream and herbal tea sellers.

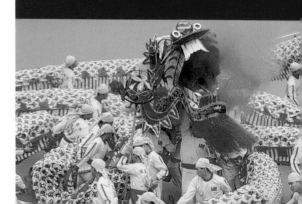

Pork fillet with Venus shells

Lombo de porco con amelijoas

500 g shellfish (preferably
Venus shells), washed
400 g pork fillet, diced
200 ml white wine
1 onion, finely chopped
2 bay leaves
12 cloves garlic, chopped
300 g potatoes, cooked
salt and pepper

1 Fry the meat in 4 tbs olive oil, then
   add the garlic, potato, bay leaves
   and onion.
2 Add the wine and simmer for
   10 minutes before adding the shellfish.
3 Cover the pan and bring to the boil.
4 Season and serve.

Portugal

In the narrow, winding streets of Portuguese working-class areas the air is heavy with the aroma of garlic. It is a flavouring the Portuguese like to use lavishly in their cooking. They like to begin their evening meal with a generous helping of Venus shells, cooked with sautéed garlic and a few sprigs of mint or coriander. An essential addition is piri piri, a very hot red pepper sauce from Angola. The combination of meat and shellfish, as in this lombo de porco con amelijoas, is not unusual in Portuguese cuisine. The strong flavours of this dish are washed down after the meal with a fine port, preferably served with a small cheese board.

Tuna with teriyaki sauce

Maguro no teriyaki

4 tuna steaks

FOR THE TERIYAKI SAUCE:
1 tsp sugar
2 tsp sake (rice wine)
or dry white wine
1 tbs mirin
(sweet rice wine)
2 tbs soy sauce
1 tbs vegetable oil
for frying
4 sprigs water cress
(for garnish)

1 Combine the ingredients for the teriyaki sauce and stir well until the sugar is dissolved.
2 Marinade the fish in the sauce for 10 minutes; turn occasionally and drain well. Retain the marinade.
3 Heat the oil in a frying pan on a moderate heat and fry the fish 2-3 minutes on one side. Turn them with care to avoid breaking them up, and fry the other side for 2 minutes. Pour off surplus oil.
4 Pour in the marinade until the fish is completely covered in sauce and fry gently for another 1-2 minutes.
5 Serve the tuna hot, garnished with water cress and grated winter radish. Add sauce from the pan as desired.

Japan

Japan is made up of a number of islands in the fish-rich Pacific. Japanese people are the largest consumers of fish in the world. This diet is one of the corner-stones of their healthy lifestyle. Japanese cookery is characterised by minimalism. "The best way to cook is not to cook" is a common saying. The traditional cuisine is based on the principle that food should be eaten as far as possible in its natural state. The Japanese diet also includes many soya products such as soy sauce and miso. Rice and fresh, fibre-rich vegetables make a Japanese meal complete. Classic preparation methods guarantee the freshness of the ingredients and preserve their natural taste, aroma and colour. In Japanese restaurants the head chefs are keen to demonstrate their cooking skills. Sushi, tempura and sashimi are prepared at the table. Restaurant guests can also often try their hand themselves. This healthy gourmet slant makes a Japanese meal into a real culinary adventure.

Mussels with chips

Mosselen met friet

4 kg mussels
1 large onion,
coarsely chopped
8 sprigs parsley
2 sprigs celery leaves
4 sprigs dill
1 small bay leaf
3 dl dry white wine
2 dl mayonnaise,
home-made if possible
1 tbs parsley,
finely chopped
1 tbs dill, finely chopped
1 tbs chives,
finely chopped
1 ½ tbs sweet pickled
gherkins, sliced very thinly
2 spring onions, slivered
salt, white pepper,
a few drops
of Tabasco, to taste

1 Rinse the mussels under cold running water. Remove any which are open or have broken shells.
2 Put the mussels in a pan. Sprinkle over the chopped onion, arrange the bouquet of unchopped herbs between them and add the wine.
3 Cover the pan and bring rapidly to the boil. Shake the pan back and forth a few times during cooking.
4 Cooking will take 7 to 8 minutes. When the shells open, the mussels are done.
5 Take the pan off the heat. Strain 1 ½ tbs of the cooking liquid into a small bowl. Leave to go cold.
6 Mix the mayonnaise with the cold cooking liquid and stir in the herbs, gherkins and spring onions. Add salt and /or pepper and Tabasco to taste.
7 Divide the mussels among deep plates or bowls and strain the remaining cooking liquid over it. Serve herb mayonnaise separately.
8 Serve with chips, knobs of salted butter and salad.

Belgium

The Belgians are inspired like no other nation by the joys of French cuisine. Belgian and French cuisine are often mentioned in the same breath, yet there are numerous Belgian specialities. Although the French claim that they invented pommes frites, they were first cooked in Belgium. It is highly likely that the Belgians living near the River Meuse in the seventeenth century were the first real chip fryers. They deep-fried their freshwater fish, but when the river froze over they resorted to potatoes. They cut them into the shape of small fishes to fry them. When there is an 'r' in the month, Belgians love to eat mussels accompanied by chips. Belgian coastal resorts and Brussels restaurants serve the mussels in the pan. Mussels are not only cooked in wine, but often in Belgian beer as well.

Pasta with mushroom sauce

Tallarines con salsa de hongos

2 rashers bacon, cubed
1 onion, chopped
150 ml sieved tomatoes
1 tomato, peeled,
deseeded and cubed
100 g ham,
cut into thin strips
100 g Spanish or other
spicy sausage, sliced
salt and pepper
150 g mushrooms,
chopped
150 ml meat stock
400 g pasta
(tagliatelli), cooked
150 g parmesan
cheese, grated

1 Fry the bacon gently in a saucepan.
   Add the onion and fry until golden
   brown.
2 Add the sieved tomatoes, the peeled
   tomato, ham, sausage, salt and
   pepper and stir well.
3 Cover the pan and simmer for
   20 minutes.
4 Add the mushrooms and stock and
   simmer, uncovered, for a further
   15 minutes.
5 Spoon a layer of pasta into a shallow,
   buttered, ovenproof dish.
6 Scatter over some of the cheese
   and spread on some of the sauce.
   Continue, a layer at a time, until all
   the ingredients are used up, ending
   with a layer of sauce.
7 Bake at 190°C for 20 minutes.

Paraguay

In the centre of South America lies Paraguay, a small country which has borders with Argentina, Bolivia and Brazil. The Paraguay river flows north to south, dividing the country into two different regions. To the west of the river lies the Chaco, a lowland plain with grasslands, sparse woodland and marshes. On the eastern side sloping hills alternate with gentle valleys and large forests. The majority of the population lives in this region. The country has two official languages: the indian Guarani language, and Spanish. The influences of both cultures can be found in the cooking. Remarkably, a small group of Italian immigrants were responsible for making pasta popular throughout Paraguay. This unique pasta dish combines Spanish sausage with Italian pasta. This dish can be found all over Paraguay, even at the roadside food stalls.

Korean pickled cabbage with fried rice

Paechu kimchi & kimchi pokkûmbab

2.5 kg Korean cabbage
(or Chinese leaves)
200 g coarse salt
500 g white radishes,
cut into strips
25 g shallot,
finely chopped
50 g spring onion,
cut into strips
60 g Korean water cress
1 tsp dried red chilli
pepper, in strips
50 g salted and fermented
shrimps
60 g garlic, finely chopped
15 g ginger,
finely chopped
1 tsp chilli powder
1 tbs sugar

1 Remove old leaves from the cabbage, insert a knife through the base of the cabbage and break the cabbage down the middle. Sprinkle the salt over the cabbage.
2 Leave to marinade for 12 hours, then rinse in cold water and drain well.
3 Add the chilli powder to the radish and mix well.
4 Put the salted and pickled shrimps, water cress and spring onion, garlic, ginger, and dried red chilli strips in a bowl and mix well with 1 tsp sugar.
5 Cut the roots from the pickled cabbage.
6 Pack the prepared vegetable and spice mixture between the layers of cabbage leaves.
7 Wrap the stuffed cabbage tightly in the outer leaves and place it in a container which is as airtight as possible.
8 Leave the kimchi to stand for 40 hours at 20°C to develop an intense flavour. (Keep any left-overs in the freezer to preserve the flavour)
9 Serve with fried rice.

Tip: Chopped dried pineapple can be used in place of sugar.

South Korea

Visitors to Seoul, the capital of South Korea, will be struck by its modernity. Skyscrapers cast their shadow over twelve-lane high-ways, which take office staff in fast cars to business destinations. Behind this hyper-modern urban façade lurks an ancient history, with palaces dating from the early Middle Ages. What Korean kings ate then is still on today's menus: the traditional kimchi, a dish consisting of roast vegetables with chilli peppers, garlic and ginger. Before kimchi appears on the table it is pickled in the traditional manner. This is an age-old method of preserving vegetables in rural areas. It was mainly the cooks in the royal palaces who devoted themselves over centuries to developing kimchi. And since Korean princes some-times had to seek marriage partners outside royal circles the refined kimchi recipes could not be kept secret from the rest of the population.

Chicken casserole with peanuts and cornmeal porridge

Sadza ne nyama ye huku

2 tbs groundnut oil
(or other vegetable oil)
2 medium onions,
finely chopped
2 cloves garlic, crushed
1 tsp salt
1 tsp black pepper
1 fresh green chilli,
deseeded and
finely chopped
450 g chicken, diced
3 large tomatoes, peeled
and finely chopped (or
tinned chopped tomatoes)
3 tbs chunky peanut butter,
home-made if possible
7 ½ dl water
1 large potato, peeled and
cut into small pieces

CORNMEAL PORRIDGE
150 g cornmeal (polenta)
3 ¾ dl cold water
pinch salt (optional)
15 g butter (optional)

1 Heat the oil in a pan and fry the onion
   until golden brown.
2 Add garlic, salt, pepper and chillies.
3 Stir fry for 2-3 minutes.
4 Add the pieces of meat and stir fry for
   5 minutes until brown on all sides.
5 Add tomatoes, peanut butter and
   7 ½ dl water.
6 Simmer for 45 minutes on a low heat
   until tender.
7 Add the potato pieces to the stew and
   cook until the potatoes are soft.
8 Serve with cornmeal porridge.

Cornmeal porridge:
1 Blend ¼of the cornmeal with ¼ dl water.
2 Put the rest of the water into a heavy pan
   and bring it to the boil.
3 Add salt and butter to taste.
4 Add the cornmeal mixture and cook for
   5 minutes on a low heat, stirring continually.
5 Add the rest of the cornmeal, cover the pan
   and boil rapidly for 3 minutes.
6 Next stir vigorously to break down any
   lumps.
7 Continue stirring until all the liquid is taken
   up and the porridge is thick but moist.
8 Cover and cook for a further 5 minutes on
   a low heat.
9 Serve immediately with the chicken stew
   with peanuts.
10 Add butter and salt to the cornmeal
   porridge according to taste.

Zimbabwe

Undulating plains, mountains and savannahs shape the landscape of Zimbabwe in East Africa. In the interior there are elephants, zebras, rhinos, antelopes and crocodiles in the wilderness of the Matopos nature reserve, and in the north, near the border with Zambia, the water rushes over the Victoria Falls. The indigenous population of Zimbabwe – consisting of Shona and Ndebele – have a society involving close links between people and obvious duties toward each other. This can also be seen in the way they eat: in groups, sitting in a circle on the ground. The staple diet of Zimbabweans consists of meat stew - nyama – and cornmeal porridge - sadze, which may be both midday and evening meal. The dish is eaten with the fingers, from a large communal bowl. This custom comes from the tradition of the Shona and Ndelebe tribes, who set great store by the sharing of food, care and responsibilities.

Tandoori thinga papad ke saath

20 peeled prawns,
size 3
3 tbs tandoori paste
8 pappadums
150 ml crème fraîche
1 tbs turmeric
2 tbs olive oil
1 tbs lemon juice
salt and pepper
100 g frisée lettuce
1 mango, cut into strips

DRESSING:
2 tbs light soy sauce
1 tbs sherry vinegar
2 tbs olive oil
1 tbs nut oil

1 Season the prawns with turmeric, salt and pepper and fry them gently in the oil.
2 Remove from pan and keep warm.
3 Remove excess oil and add the tandoori paste and crème fraîche.
4 Cook until reduced by half and season to taste with lemon juice and salt.
5 Make the dressing and use it to coat the lettuce and mango strips.
6 Take the salad and arrange it in a circle with the pappadums.
7 Place the prawns in the centre and cover them with the sauce.
8 Garnish with chives.
9 Serve with steamed rice.

India

In India, the birthplace of Buddhism and Hinduism, food and spirituality are almost in-extricably intermixed. Nomadic tribes from the Urals, who settled India long before our era, laid the foundations of the Hindu eating traditions. In their eyes the finest food was transformed into soul or spirit. Buddhism introduced principles of abstinence, sobriety and simplicity to Indian cooking. Followers of this movement laid the foundations of Indian vegetarianism. Over the centuries many cultures have influenced Indian food. The Persians, for example, brought in numerous meat and egg dishes. During the colonial period the British left their mark on the way meals were served. In the higher echelons of society, particularly, cloths gave way to tables and banana leaves were replaced by crockery. Indian dishes also began at that time to appear on European menus. Curries, particularly, like this tandoori dish, are popular and familiar all over the Western world.

Lamb stew with vegetables

Irish stew

FOR 4 TO 6 PEOPLE
1 ½ kg neck or shoulder of lamb
1 celeriac
4 onions
4 carrots
3 leeks
1 bouquet garni (thyme, parsley, bay leaf)
salt, black pepper
6 potatoes
100 g white cabbage
Worcester sauce
1 bunch of parsley, chopped

1 Remove the fat from the meat, bone it and cut it into cubes (retain the bones)
2 Bring the meat to the boil in a pan of cold salted water and then rinse it off.
3 Clean and chop the celeriac, onions, carrots and leeks.
4 Place the vegetables with the meat, bone and bouquet garni in another pan, season with salt and pepper.
5 Cover the ingredients with water and stew for 60 minutes.
6 Skim off the froth from time to time.
7 Peel and cut up the potatoes, and add them to the pan to simmer for a further 30 minutes.
8 Wash the white cabbage and chop it finely.
9 Add the cabbage to the pan for the last 5 minutes of the cooking time.
10 Remove the bone and bouquet garni.
11 Season the stew to taste with Worcester sauce and add the chopped parsley.

Ireland

The Celts, ancestors of the Irish, were a race of storytellers. They sang of their heroic deeds: tales which were passed from generation to generation in centuries of oral tradition. So a rich culture developed of sagas, legends and stories. Thanks to this tradition much is also known about the traditional diet of the Irish. For example there are stories about the potato, which was the staple diet of the Irish from the sixteenth to the nineteenth century. According to tradition, the privateer Walter Raleigh introduced the potato to Ireland, where it flourished in the damp climate. Around the seventeenth century the Irish consumed five kilos of potatoes a day. However, this changed in 1845. The potato harvest failed, and a disastrous famine followed. After this the Irish broadened their horizons; they grew more varies crops on their fertile land. New ingredients were added to the traditional potato dishes. Around 150 years ago this famous Irish stew would have been eaten without the lamb and vegetables.

Grilled chicken Filippino

Inihaw na manok

125 ml pineapple juice
150 g brown sugar
4 tbs soy sauce
2 tsp white vinegar
1 tsp garlic, finely chopped
1 tsp ginger,
finely chopped
1 tbs honey
¼ tsp freshly ground black
pepper
1.25-1.5 kg chicken,
in ready-to-serve pieces

1 Mix the pineapple juice with the brown sugar, soy sauce, vinegar, garlic, ginger, honey and black pepper.
2 Marinate the chicken in this and leave it in the refrigerator for at least four hours, preferably overnight
3 Grill the chicken pieces over charcoal or under a grill until they are cooked and golden brown.
4 Baste the chicken with the marinade regularly while grilling.

The Philippines

The Philippines, an archipelago lying between the Pacific and the South China Sea, is a melting pot of different cultures. Influences from Malaysia, China, Spain and America in particular have contributed to a flexible cuisine, with many dishes having both oriental and Western origins. The popularity of noodles and rice is due to the Chinese, who once traded there. Spanish conquerors introduced dishes which well-off Filipinos made for festive occasions: Spanish stews or guisados became particularly popular. Down the centuries dishes have been created which owe their origins to China but now have Spanish names. Experts consider that the Filipinos have adapted foods from other countries so as to give them a character of their own. Filipinos like Asian flavourings such as ginger, garlic and onion, and they also like contrasting tastes, as in this chicken dish, which blends bitter, sour and sweet flavours.

Breast of duck with apple

Friptura de rata cu mere coapte

4 boned duck breasts
4 green apples, peeled
and cut into segments
4 tbs sugar
1 tbs grated lemon rind
2 tbs lemon juice
1 tsp salt

1 Rub the duck with salt and make diagonal cuts on the fatty side.
2 Heat a pan on medium heat, sprinkle in the sugar and fry the duck in this, fatty side first.
3 After about 5 minutes turn it over and fry the other side for 3 minutes, then add the apple and lemon.
4 Put the whole mixture in an ovenproof dish with the fatty side up and bake in the oven for 10 minutes at 180°C.

Romania

Romania, the country of the Carpathians, the Danube delta and the Black Sea, has a wealth of natural food sources. The Carpathians, in the heart of the country, are covered in woods where deer, wild boar, wolves and even bears roam. Mountain ramblers returning hungry from a long expedition can tuck into sour soups (ciorbas), salads and game dishes. The Danube offers a plentiful supply of freshwater fish, which the Romanians have a special way of preparing: freshly caught carp are grilled on sticks over a wood fire. At the mouth of the Danube the river splits into numerous arms forming the Danube delta. This watery wilderness area on the north coast of the Black Sea is a true paradise for birdwatchers, visited by pelicans, ibises, whooper swans and mandarin ducks. The Danube delta is an ideal place to enjoy poultry dishes, which go extremely well with the Romanian wines from this area.

Chilli crab

Cili ketma

4 medium-sized fresh crabs
1 tbs fresh ginger, finely chopped
3 garlic cloves, finely chopped
4 fresh red or green chilli peppers, finely chopped
1 tsp shrimp paste
4 tbs oil
2 tbs tomato paste
1 tbs fish sauce
1 tbs light soy sauce
1 tsp sugar

1 Ask the fishmonger for four fresh, cleaned crabs with theclaws broken off.
2 Chop each crab into four pieces and put it on one side.
3 Grind the ginger, garlic and chilli peppers to a paste in a pestle and mortar and mix in the shrimp paste.
4 Heat the oil in a wok and sauté the paste in it.
5 Stir in the tomato paste and 2 tbs water.
6 Add the crab pieces and mix well.
7 Add the fish sauce, soy sauce and sugar and stir, making sure all the crab pieces are covered in sauce.
8 Spoon onto a dish and serve.

Singapore

The palm-fringed beaches along the Singaporean coast are teeming with little restaurants serving a wide variety of hot, spicy fish dishes. The custom here is to eat with your hands, which, the Singaporeans claims, brings out the flavour. There is an etiquette, however: you only use the fingertips of the right hand, keeping your palm clean. You wash your hands before and after the meal for reasons of politeness and hygiene. In the higher-class establishments the waiter places a finger bowl on the table for you to use, but in the 'banana leaf restaurants' you will find rows of washbasins with soap. Connoisseurs claim that this crab chilli, Singapore's most popular dish, is particularly tasty when eaten with the fingers. Although the name suggests that it is scorching hot, the tomato paste and sugar tone down the taste of the peppers

Okra soup with fried bananas

Sòpi di guyambo & banana asá

200 g salt beef,
soaked overnight
1.5 litres beef stock
200 g red mullet
or snapper
100 g shrimps
200 g okras,
sliced into thin rings
4 green peppers
2 tomatoes,
chopped in half
2 plantains
1-2 tbs oil for frying

1 Simmer the salt beef in the stock for
  90 minutes.
2 Add the fish, whole peppers, sliced
  okras and tomatoes and allow to
  simmer for 10 minutes.
3 Heat the oil in a frying pan, chop
  the plantains in half and fry them in
  the hot oil.
4 Serve the soup in bowls with the fried
  bananas on the side.

Netherlands Antilles

The Netherlands Antilles comprises the Caribbean islands of Curaçao, Bonaire, Saba, Sint Eustatius and Saint Martin; the island of Aruba was also included until 1986, when it achieved separate status. The roots of Antillean cuisine lie with the Amerindian population, who ate mainly fish, corn, "brown beans" (a type of haricot bean), sweet potatoes and cassava. The Spaniards brought in pork, mangoes, lemons and olives. In their wake millions of slaves came into the Caribbean to work on the sugar cane plantations. They introduced the natives to Creole cuisine with its banana dishes, funchi (corn bread) and guyambo (okra). Sòpi di guyambo is a mixture of Amerindian, Spanish and Creole influences.

Loin of pork in stout with duchess potatoes

Schweinelende in Dunkelbier mit Herzoginkartoffeln

500 g pork fillet
2 tbs butter
salt & pepper
1 tbs caraway seed
¼ litre stout
¼ litre beef stock
100 g crème fraîche

DUCHESS POTATOES:
500 g potatoes
100 g butter
salt
nutmeg
3 egg yolks

1 Brown the meat on both sides in the butter, season with salt, pepper and caraway seed.
2 Add the stout and the beef stock and simmer with the lid on for about 20 minutes until cooked.
3 Reduce the gravy and mix in the crème fraîche.
4 Boil the potatoes and mash them with the egg yolks and butter, season with nutmeg and salt.
5 Pipe rosettes of the mashed potato and brown them under the grill.

Germany

German cooking used to be dominated by heavy peasant-style dishes like sauerkraut, pig's trotters, stews and sausages, but nowadays the Germans are revealing themselves to be gourmets with an interest in healthy ingredients and ecological produce. There is no typical German cuisine: ingredients and methods differ from one Land to another. But potatoes and pork are still very popular in most regions, even if the Germans have far more different ways of cooking them than they used to. A popular potato dish is Reibekuchen or potato pancake, and many dishes are served with potato salad or mashed potato. It is not surprising that the Germans like to cook their dishes in beer, since Germany has a great beer tradition. There are annual festivals like the Munich Beer Festival (Oktoberfest), where it is drunk from one-litre tankards. This pork dish with stout gives a new twist to traditional ingredients.

Barbecued shrimps

Aussie shrimp on the barbie

12 prawns, peeled but
with their heads
and tails on
2 tbs butter
juice of 2 oranges
2 tbs sherry
1 tbs grated orange peel
2 spring onions,
finely chopped
2 cm fresh ginger, chopped

1 Soak 12 long wooden skewers in water for 30 minutes.
2 Skewer each prawn lengthwise.
3 Put all the other ingredients in a saucepan and simmer on low heat, stirring until all the butter has melted.
4 Dip the skewered prawns in the orange sauce and put them on an oiled rack about 10 cm above the glowing charcoal.
5 Sprinkle them generously with sauce and grill for about 2 minutes.
6 Turn them over and sprinkle them again, then grill for another 2 minutes.
7 Keep sprinkling and turning until they are pink and cooked.
8 Take them off the heat immediately; overgrilling makes them tough.
9 Use the remaining sauce as a dip for the prawns.

Australia

Australia, an island continent between the Pacific and the Indian Ocean, has an extremely mixed population. The aboriginals were the original inhabitants, but they have been joined by a huge number of immigrants from Great Britain, Ireland and, later, Greece, Italy, Yugoslavia and Lebanon. The great influx has caused major changes in traditional eating habits. The Greeks, for instance, added variety and subtlety to the menu. A host of foreign restaurants have opened in the cities in recent decades. Despite the wide variety of eating habits, almost all the island-dwellers love barbecues. Sometimes these are formal occasions, with a whole lamb roasting on a spit and elegantly dressed diners sipping champagne. But there's nothing to beat an evening sitting round a camp fire on the beach with family or friends. Fresh fish you have caught yourself is best for an Aussie barbie.

T-bone steak with pepper and paprika salad

Biftec con ensalade de aji y pimiento

PEPPER AND PAPRIKA SALAD:
8 medium-hot green chilli
peppers
1 red pepper
1 red onion, chopped
2 beef tomatoes, skinned,
deseeded and cubed
1 garlic clove, chopped
1 tbs lemon juice
1 tsp salt
4 tbs olive oil

1 Roast the chilli peppers on a barbecue or under a grill until the skins turn black, cover with foil and leave to rest for 10 minutes, take off the skins and finely chop the flesh.
2 Do the same with the red pepper.
3 Mix the chilli peppers and red pepper with the other salad ingredients and leave it to stand for at least 30 minutes.
4 Barbecue the T-bone steak as you like it.

Argentina

The Argentinian equivalent of barbecue is asado, a word that refers not only to the method of cooking but also to the food itself and the fiesta surrounding it. The whole ritual is played out around an Argentinian grill, a set of large iron spits over a wood fire. Asados can take place anywhere, on balconies, in an open space in town, right out in the country, or at an elegant dinner for a select company. The most famous barbecue is that of the Gaucho, where whole ribs are grilled. Taking the ribs off the spits is a job for the parilleros, the asado experts: only they know when the meat is cooked.

Chicken with green curry and coconut

Gaeng kheow wan gai

2 tbs olive oil
2 onions
1 tbs fresh ginger
600 g boned breast
of chicken
200 ml unsweetened
coconut milk
150 ml chicken stock
1 tbs Thai green curry
paste
1 bunch fresh basil
1 tbs fresh coriander
200 g mangetout
2 spring onions
rice

1 Boil the rice.
2 Chop the onions and fresh ginger and
   finely slice the spring onions.
3 Cut the chicken into strips.
4 Finely chop the coriander and basil.
5 Heat the oil in a medium-sized pan over
   medium heat. Fry the onion and ½ tbs
   ginger in it for about a minute.
6 Add the chicken and fry it for about
   3 minutes until golden brown.
7 Transfer the mixture to a bowl.
8 Put the coconut milk, stock and green
   curry paste in the pan.
9 Mix until smooth.
10 Add 1 tbs basil, coriander and ½ tbs
   ginger and bring the sauce to the boil.
11 Turn down the heat and simmer for
   about 7 minutes until thick.
12 Add the mangetout and onions.
13 Return the chicken and vegetable
   mixture to the pan.
14 Simmer for about 5 minutes until the
   chicken is cooked.
15 Season with salt and pepper.
16 Serve the rice on plates and pour over
   the chicken and vegetable mixture.
17 Garnish with the remaining basil.

Thailand

Thailand is often described as an earthly paradise. Mountainous country and fertile river valleys dominate in the north. The flat land in the centre is one of the richest rice-growing areas in the world, alternating between paddy fields, orchards and vegetable gardens. Rice and fish are the principal ingredients on the Thai menu, prepared in a refined manner with a selection of herbs and spices, vegetables and sauces (e.g. coriander, aubergines and fish sauce). Thai cuisine, like Thai art, is notable for its attention to detail. The country's produce is collected and delicately combined into a harmonious blend of strong and subtle, sweet and sour flavours. Thai cooking involves more than just following a recipe: to get the balance of flavours just right it is essential to taste the food as you go along. Anyone who enjoys experimenting in the kitchen is guaranteed to enjoy making this Thai curry.

Squid curry

Squid de calman

1 tbs coriander seed
1 tsp cumin seed
1 shallot, finely chopped
2 garlic cloves, peeled
1 cm fresh ginger, finely chopped
1 stalk lemon grass, finely chopped
3 fresh red chilli peppers, deseeded
2 fresh green peppers
4 tbs fresh coriander leaves
1 tbs curry powder
2 tbs corn oil
250 g tomatoes, peeled, deseeded and chopped into quarters
250 ml thick coconut milk
250 ml fish stock
500 g fresh baby squid, cleaned and sliced into rings
salt & pepper

1 Roast the coriander seed and cumin seed for about 3 minutes in a pan on low heat. Put it in the food processor.
2 Add the shallot, garlic, ginger, lemon grass, 2 tbs coriander leaves, red chilli peppers, curry powder and salt and blend into a paste.
3 Heat the corn oil in a pan and fry the curry paste for about 5 minutes until it smells fragrant.
4 Add the tomatoes and cook for 5-6 minutes.
5 Add the coconut milk and fish stock and stir until the mixture takes on an oily glow. To improve the flavour, leave the mixture to stand for a while.
6 Add the baby squid, salt and fresh green peppers to the pan and bring back to the boil, then reduce the heat and simmer for 5 minutes until the squid are tender. Add salt and pepper.
7 Sprinkle the rest of the fresh coriander leaves over the squid and serve immediately with boiled or steamed rice.

Mauritius

Mauritius is an archipelago in the Indian Ocean surrounded by magnificent coral reefs with a motley collection of sea life. The island-dwellers, who down the centuries have blown in from all points of the compass, are no less colourful than the fish on the reef - descendants of Portuguese, Dutch and British colonials, African slaves, Chinese traders and Indian labourers live here jumbled up together. Variety is the watchword on the islands: bastardized languages and dialects create an exotic cacophony of sound, and at pavement cafes waiters serve Yorkshire pudding at one table and an exotic fresh fish curry at another without batting an eyelid, against a background of Creole music. This baby squid curry is the delicious result of a melting pot of different cultures.

Roast pork with ginger and honey

Cha siu

500 g pork
100 g honey

FOR THE MARINADE:
2 slices ginger,
finely chopped
1 garlic clove,
finely chopped
2 shallots, finely chopped
2 tbs light soy sauce
1 tsp salt
5 tbs sugar
1 tbs Mei Kuei Lu (Chinese
clear distilled liquor)
1 tsp ng heung fan
(five-spice powder)
2 tsp red food colouring
(optional)

1 Cut the pork into 2cm-thick slices.
2 Mix all the ingredients for the
marinade and marinate the pork in it
for two hours.
3 Stir the honey with 4 tbs water in a
small saucepan on low heat until it
liquefies.
4 Preheat the oven to 150°C.
5 Scrape the marinade off the pork and
place the slices on a greased rack in
the oven.
6 After 15 minutes, place under a hot
grill, at least 10 cm from the heat
(oven grill: 250°C).
7 Turn the meat over after 5-7 minutes,
turn down the heat a little and grill the
other side, again for 5-7 minutes (oven
grill: 225°C).
8 Spread clear honey over both sides of
the meat and grill it for another minute
on each side (225°C).
9 Remove the meat from the grill, allow
to cool for a few minutes, then cut into
narrow strips.

China

China, the largest country on the
planet, is a world in itself. The enormous diversity of landscape, climate
and customs is reflected in Chinese
food culture. In the north, along the
Yellow River, the landscape is rough,
brown and rolling: the food is sub-
stantial and spicy, with yellow wheat,
millet and soya beans. Around the
Yangtse, in the south, the land-scape
is green and lush: here the dominant
foods are white rice and a wide variety of vegetables, which are prepared with refinement. There are four
main regional styles of Chinese cuisine: those of Peking and Shandong;
Shanghai; Szechuan; and Canton and
Guangzhou. Cha siu is a Cantonese
speciality. Typical of Cantonese cuisine are fresh ingredients, fine sauces
and imported flavourings such as
lemon and curry. Cantonese chefs are
past masters in the roasting of meat.
With this recipe every-one can try to
follow in their footsteps.

Cheese fondue

Chäsfondü

1 garlic clove
400 g Gruyere cheese
200 g Emmental cheese
300 ml white wine
1 tsp lemon juice
2 tsp cornflour
100 ml cherry brandy
black pepper
nutmeg, grated
white bread, cubed

1 Rub an earthenware cooking pot with garlic.
2 Grate or finely chop the two cheeses.
3 Bring the wine, lemon juice and cheese to the boil, stirring constantly.
4 Mix the cornflour with the cherry brandy, blend this into the cheese mixture and season with pepper and nutmeg.
5 Boil the mixture briefly until it is smooth and creamy.
6 Place the pot on a spirit stove or hotplate on the table.
7 Let the fondue continue simmering while eating, stirring it occasionally so that it remains smooth and creamy.
8 To eat, spear the pieces of bread on a long fork and dip them in the fondue.

Tip: if the fondue is too thin, add a little more grated cheese; if it gets too thick, dilute it with wine.

Switzerland

Switzerland is particularly famous for its independence and neutrality vis-à-vis the rest of the world, and this self-assurance is reflected in Swiss cuisine: the Swiss have borrowed very few dishes from their French, German or Italian neighbours. True Swiss cuisine is best found in small country establishments in the mountains, where milk, cheese, meat and local crops are made into dishes. Swiss cheese owes its high quality to fertile meadows, clean Alpine air and healthy cattle. Swiss Emmental cheese, which has a two thousand-year tradition behind it, is world-famous nowadays. The best-known Swiss cheese recipe is the fondue from the Canton of Neuchâtel (Neuenburg), whose main ingredients are two cheeses - usually Emmental and Gruyere - and white wine. Fondue recipes vary from one Canton to another, as each region is proud of its own cheeses.

Provençal fish soup

Bouillabaisse

SERVES 6
8 kg Mediterranean fish
(racasse - a bony rock
fish - and at least six other
varieties: weever, monkfish,
gurnard, whiting, bass,
saint-pierre; crab and spiny
lobster if available)
2 large onions,
peeled and chopped
2 tbs olive oil
4 tomatoes,
peeled and chopped
1 bouquet garni
1 strip orange peel
4 garlic cloves, crushed
1 g saffron threads
freshly ground pepper
salt
slices of dark coarse
bread, toasted
(1.5 cm thick)
750 g potatoes, cut into
pieces (if desired)

ROUILLE
(GARLIC MAYONNAISE):
2 garlic cloves
2 red chilli peppers,
cleaned
cayenne pepper
1 pinch saffron
2 tbs white bread
(without crust), soaked in
chicken stock
1.5 tbs olive oil

1 Clean the fish, crab and spiny lobster.
2 Separate the firm-fleshed fish (racasse, weever, monkfish, gurnard, crab and spiny lobster) from the soft-fleshed fish (whiting, bass, saint-pierre).
3 Sweat the onions in 8 tbs olive oil in a large pan.
4 Add the tomatoes to the onions.
5 Add the bouquet garni, orange peel, garlic cloves and saffron.
6 Season the fish with salt and pepper. Place the firm-fleshed fish on top of the vegetables in the pan and sprinkle with the remaining olive oil. Cook gently on low heat for 10 minutes, then carefully pour in boiling water until it just covers the fish. Adjust the seasoning.
7 If you wish you can cook pieces of potato slowly with the fish.
8 Bring the bouillabaisse to the boil, let it boil on high heat for 5 minutes, then add the soft-fleshed fish and boil for another 5-7 minutes: the oil and stock must combine.
9 Place a slice of bread in each bowl and pour over the fish stock. Serve the spiny lobster, crab, fish and rouille separately.

Rouille:
1 Peel the garlic cloves and crush them with the chilli peppers in a pestle and mortar. Season the mixture with cayenne pepper and saffron.
2 Squeeze the stock out of the bread and mix it into the rouille.
3 Beat the olive oil into the rouille, adding it drop by drop until the sauce is as thick as mustard.

France

Lovers of French cuisine cannot do without Provence, the region with the best vegetables, the strongest herbs and spices, the finest garlic and the liveliest wines. The cuisine is at least as colourful, rich and varied as the landscape. Bouillabaisse, the famous rich fish soup, perfectly exemplifies the generosity of Provençal cuisine. Although this regional speciality is sometimes referred to as 'golden soup', it has simple origins. The word bouillabaisse is derived from bouillir (to boil) and baisse (refuse). Fishermen used to make their soup from the remnants of their catches, adding any unsold fish. There are many variants along the Mediterranean coast. The French tacitly assume that soup can only be called bouillabaisse if it contains at least six different kinds of fish. Bouillabaisse tastes best with marette (country bread) spread with rouille (spicy garlic mayonnaise), especially after a day at the seaside.

Goulash

Gulyásleves

500 g stewing beef
500 g raw potatoes, cubed
50 g butter
2 onions, finely chopped
2 garlic cloves
2 tsp paprika
5 small carrots
chopped parsley
2 tomatoes or 1 tbs tomato paste
1.5 litres water

FOR THE CSIPETKE (CROUTONS):
2 tbs flour
1 egg
pinch of salt
2 tbs water

1 Sweat the chopped onions and garlic in the butter until golden yellow.
2 Stir in the paprika and add the beef and tomatoes.
3 Gradually add hot water until the meat is covered.
4 Simmer until almost cooked.
5 Add the carrots and raw cubed potatoes.
6 Add the rest of the water.
7 Simmer for another 15-20 minutes.
8 Meanwhile, make a dough from the ingredients for the csipetke.
9 Pull off small pieces of the hard dough and add them to the soup 5 minutes before serving.
10 Season the soup and serve with chopped parsley.

Hungary

Gulyásleves, the Hungarian national dish, originated in the kitchens of the Gulya, the Hungarian shepherds who roamed the wide expanse of the pustas. They made the soup on an open fire in a bogrács, the cast iron kettle brought in by horsemen from the Carpathian Basin. This traditional cooking pot is still used in traditional Hungarian restaurants and farm kitchens. There are many variants of Gulyásleves using pork, mutton or beef, but paprika, onion and cream give it its typical Hungarian flavour. It can be served as a soup or stew.

Asparagus with ham and eggs

Asperges met ham en eieren

SERVES 4
2 kg asparagus
(shoots of equal thickness)
salt
1 tsp sugar
8 eggs
200 g ham, sliced
4 sprigs parsley,
finely chopped
150 g butter
nutmeg

1 Peel the asparagus from top to bottom using a peeler.
2 Cut off about 2 cm from the bottoms.
3 Make the asparagus into bunches of 6-8 shoots, with the tips together, and tie them up at each end with string. Keep them under water until you need them.
4 Bring plenty of water to the boil with salt and sugar in a broad, shallow pan, put in the bunches of asparagus and boil for about 10 minutes until cooked.
5 Hard-boil the eggs (10 minutes).
6 Roll up the slices of ham (first cut them in half if necessary).
7 Cool the eggs in cold running water, peel them and cut them in half.
8 Melt the butter in a small saucepan on low heat.
9 Remove the asparagus from the pan using a skimmer and place it on a clean tea towel.
10 Cut the strings and lay the asparagus, with the tips together, on a serving dish. Garnish with parsley.
11 Place the ham rolls and half eggs alongside the asparagus. Serve the melted butter and nutmeg separately.
12 Serve with boiled new potatoes.

The Netherlands

Although many Dutch families still sit down at six o'clock in the evening sharp to eat mashed potatoes mixed with carrots, endive or curly kale with sausage, there has been a major shift in Dutch food culture in recent decades. New ingredients and methods have been adopted following holidays in Europe and further afield, and immigrant styles of cooking have been a source of culinary inspiration. The Dutch are increasingly revealing themselves to be gourmets who enjoy cooking and wining and dining with friends until late at night. In the south of the country this 'Burgundian' lifestyle has been the norm for quite some time, probably due to Belgian and French influence, the milder climate and the excellent pro-duce of the Limburg region, including asparagus. The 'white gold' tastes best in spring, when it has just come out of the ground.

Sautéed Baltic herring with mashed potato and dill

Pastettu silakka, perunamuusi ja tillivoi

SERVES 4
12 herrings,
washed and cleaned
60 g flour
salt & pepper
butter for frying

MASHED POTATO:
300 g mashed potato
20 ml cream
80 g butter
80 salt & pepper
1 small bunch dill,
chopped
1 lemon, sliced

1 Season the herrings with salt and pepper and roll them in the flour and fry them in the butter. Keep them hot.

Mashed potato:
1 Mix all the ingredients.
2 Serve the mashed potato with the herrings, dill and lemon, not forgetting the ice-cold koskenkorva (the local schnapps).

Finland

The Finnish landscape is mainly woods and lakes. Wood is a major export, and a source of inspiration for Finnish furniture designers. Finnish interior design is famous throughout the world. Wooden saunas are another Finnish speciality: everywhere on the banks of the lakes are wooden huts where people sit and sweat at their leisure before jumping into the ice-cold water to cool off. Taking saunas is a favourite pastime, and goes with eating and drinking. On a clear midsummer night, when the sun stays above the horizon, the sauna ritual can go on interminably. In between taking saunas people eat in the open air. There is often a hot and cold buffet, including the mandatory crayfish. Herring from the Baltic is another popular dish, and with it the Fins like to drink koskenkorva, a strong Finnish liquor. They sweat off the alcohol in the sauna, then go back to enjoy another drink.

Peppers stuffed with ewe's milk cheese

Palneni chuski s ovche sirene

4 red peppers
6 eggs
250 g ewe's milk cheese
parsley, finely chopped
150 g breadcrumbs
2 tbs butter
salt & pepper

1 Cut off the tops of the peppers and take out the seeds.
2 Mix the crumbled cheese with the eggs and 100 g breadcrumbs and season.
3 Stuff the peppers with the mixture, cover them with flakes of butter and sprinkle over the rest of the breadcrumbs; place in an ovenproof dish.
4 Bake them in the oven for 45 minutes at 170°C.
5 Sprinkle them with finely chopped parsley.

Bulgaria

The Bulgarians were originally a Turkish people who camped on the banks of the Volga. In the seventh century they got together with Slavs to found a country between the Danube and the Balkan Mountains - Bulgaria. A mountainous Balkan country on the Black Sea, it has a pure, simple cuisine with strong flavours. Because of the country's situation and history, Bulgarian cuisine combines elements from Slav, Greek and Turkish cooking. The dishes are made from natural local produce in season. Fresh vegetables, herbs and spices, peppers and garlic provide the strong flavours typical of the East European cuisine. Many dishes feature paprika peppers, which are used not only in salads and soups but also in cheese and egg dishes. They are often rounded off with creamy Bulgarian yoghurt, now popular throughout the world. Bulgarian wines are also gaining recognition internationally: a red wine from the Sungurlare valley makes a perfect accompaniment to this paprika dish.

Fried mackerel with nuts and red peppers

Pepesan ikan

4 keremi nuts, chopped
4 mackerel
1 tbs salt
5 tbs oil
2 onions, sliced into
half rings
6 garlic cloves
4 red chilli peppers, with
or without seeds, chopped
4 leaves jeruk purut
(lime leaves)
2 stalks sereh
(lemon grass), crushed
juice of 1 lime

1 Cut off the head of the mackerel.
2 Rub the mackerel with salt and brown
them in the oil for 2 minutes on
each side.
3 Add the nuts, onion, garlic and peppers
and fry briefly, then take the pan off
the heat.
4 Add lime juice, jeruk purut and
lemon grass.
5 Place each mackerel on a piece of
aluminium foil and spread it with the
remaining ingredients.
6 Close the foil over the fish and bake in
the oven for 40-50 minutes at 150°C.

Indonesia

Indonesia comprises over 18,000 islands with a total of 190 inhabitants.

The island of Java is the political and economic centre of the archipelago. It has magnificent Buddhist and Hindu temples for visitors to admire, for example Borobudur and Prambanan. Islam has also left its mark, not least on the food culture. The Javanese of the Sultanate of Yokyakarta excel in preparing special dishes for the 'community feast' or selamatan, with mountains of yellow rice, roast chicken, and soya beans and shrimps fried in spicy coconut milk as the highlights. The best way for a culinary explorer to sample Javanese food is to go out on the streets, which are full of little restaurants (warungs) serving a colourful variety of dishes. This pepesan ikan is from a warung in Yokyakarta: the street vendors serve it on a banana leaf.

Desserts

Caramelised pineapple

Gekarameliseerde pynappel

2 pineapples
1 tbs cayenne pepper
2 tbs fresh ginger, chopped
6 vanilla pods
80 g demerara sugar

1 Peel the pineapples and cut them in half.
2 Lay the two halves round side up on a buttered oven dish.
3 Rub them in with pepper and ginger and stick pieces of vanilla pod into the surface.
4 Sprinkle with sugar and allow to caramelise in the oven at 180°C for 30 minutes.
5 Serve the pineapple with pineapple ice cream, coconut or chocolate flakes.

South Africa

The population of South African forms a kaleidoscope of different colours, religions and cultural heritages, which have created a wide diversity of lifestyles and culinary traditions. "Boerenkos" or farm food embraces the hearty cooking of the countryside. Cape Malay denotes the culinary heritage of the former Indian and Malaysian slave population brought to South Africa by colonial Europeans. In the course of time Cape Malay has evolved into a sophisticated culinary style with a wide variety of piquant flavours to be found in its many curry dishes. The huge variety and wealth of influences means South Africa has no obvious single culinary tradition. But one thing common to the country's many cooking styles is their use of fresh ingredients from the fertile South African countryside, like pineapple for example.

Chocolate pecan pie

Chocolate pecan pie

250 g flour
125 g icing sugar
150 g unsalted butter,
softened
150 g chocolate,
finely chopped
4 eggs
230 ml dark corn syrup
(or maple syrup)
pith of one vanilla pod
225 g shelled pecan nuts

1 Whisk the eggs with the sugar and vanilla to a stiff froth.
2 Melt the butter with the chocolate and 200 ml syrup.
3 Add this to the egg mixture and blend in the flour.
4 Pour into a round (28 cm) cake tin and bake the pie in the oven at 170°C for 20 minutes.
5 Stir the pecan nuts into 30 ml syrup and spread the mixture on the tart.
6 Return to the oven and bake for another 10 minutes.

United States

Among the culinary traditions of the US the state of California stands out in every respect. This fertile state is renowned for its regional cooking, stemming from English, Scottish, Irish, French, native Indian and Creole traditions. New Orleans is the culinary centre of the south. Typical dishes here have emerged from a refreshing synthesis of the French talent for subtle blends of flavours, the Spanish love of strong aromas, native Indian knowledge of root vegetables and herbs and the culinary skills of the early settlers. Pecan pie is another specialty of southern cooking. Pecan nuts grow wild in both California and Texas.

Coffee dessert with banana and yoghurt

Sobremesa de Café com banana e iogurte

6 bananas
2 tbs instant coffee
4 tbs rum
3 tbs demerara sugar
150 ml cream
pith of one vanilla pod
2 tbs icing sugar
4 tbs roasted nuts,
finely chopped

1 Peel and slice 2 bananas and puree
  them in a blender with the demerara
  sugar, rum and instant coffee.
2 Whisk the cream stiff with the icing
  sugar and vanilla.
3 Cut the remaining 4 bananas in half.
4 Serve them with the rum sauce and
  cream, and sprinkle with chopped nuts.

Brazil

Brazilian cooking is as diverse as the country's climate and intermingling of cultures.Native Indian, African and Portuguese traditions in particular have left their mark on the country's culinary heritage. Brazil is the world's leading producer of coffee. According to legend this was thanks to a colonel who in 1727 was assigned by the Brazilian government to settle a dispute between French and Dutch settlers in Guiana. There he had an affair with the wife of a local governor. When he left to return to Brazil she give him a bouquet of flowers in which she had concealed seeds and cuttings of the coffee plant. This bouquet is said to have marked the beginnings of the Brazilian coffee industry. Coffee is a wonderful basis for mouth-watering desserts. The nuts and banana combine to give it an exotic aroma. Yoghurt can be substituted for the cream to reduce the calorie count.

Meringue with caramel sauce

Pavlova

MERINGUE:
4 egg whites
4 tbs cold water
1 tbs white wine vinegar
1 pinch of salt
250 g sugar
1 tsp vanilla sugar
4 tbs cornflour
1 tbs oil

FILLING:
100 g hazelnuts,
roasted and chopped
1–2 tbs nut liqueur
400 ml cream,
whisked to a soft peak
400 g mixed berries
juice of 1 lemon

CARAMEL SAUCE:
250 g sugar
250 g cream

Meringue:
1 Whisk the egg whites with a pinch of salt to a stiff peak.
2 Continue to whisk while gradually adding the water and then the sugar.
3 Then add the vanilla, vinegar and cornflour.
4 Oil 2 baking tins size 12 by 24 cm.
5 Divide the whisked egg whites into two equal portions on to the baking tins, smoothing one down flat and hollowing out the centre of the other, and bake them in the oven at 150°C for about 35 minutes.

Filling:
1 Blend all the ingredients for the filling.
2 Spread some of the mixture on the flat meringue base, then lay the hollowed meringue on top and spoon the remaining filling into the hollow.

Caramel sauce:
1 Heat the sugar in a pan without stirring until it caramelises in about 5 minutes.
2 Add the cream and leave on a low heat until it has dissolved, then allow to cool.
3 Coat the Pavlova with the caramel sauce and serve.

New Zealand

Alongside a modern gastronomic culture stemming from a range of influences, the older generation of New Zealanders in particular still cling to a truly pioneering cooking tradition. When the first British immigrants arrived on these islands in the 18th and 19th centuries they had to adjust to a new and challenging environment. They ate large quantities of preserved and pickled foods and built up stores for difficult times, using the generous quantities of vegetables and fruit growing wild as well as the crops cultivated in their own gardens. The New Zealand tastes and cooking methods of that pioneering age have meanwhile become interwoven with the aromas and culinary methods of all the countries bordering the Pacific. This tradition is now termed Pacific Rim cooking and is based primarily on fish, fruit (papayas, bananas and blue-berries) and coconut. Fruit appears not only in desserts by also in many main course dishes, which often incorporate kiwis. But with desserts like the Pavlova, New Zealand cooks aspire to the pinnacle of culinary art.

Cake with poppy seed and stewed fruit

Makiwnyk

CAKE:
80 g poppy seed
180 ml soya milk or water
2 tbs cornflour
6 tbs oil
60 g unrefined sugar
pith of 1 vanilla pod
grated rind of ½ a
lime or orange
250 g flour
1 tsp cinnamon
1 ½ tsp baking powder

GLAZE:
juice of 1 lime
1 tbs sugar

1 Sprinkle the poppy seed into a large bowl of soya milk or water and allow to stand for 1 hour.
2 Stir the cornflour, oil, sugar, vanilla and grated rind into the poppy seed and liquid, mixing thoroughly.
3 Mix the dry ingredients together in a separate bowl.
4 Stir the dry ingredients into the liquid mix, blending well.
5 Turn the dough into a lightly oiled bread or cake tin and bake the cake in the oven at 175°C for 45 minutes.
6 Add the sugar to the lime juice in a small pan and heat until dissolved, then use this to glaze the cake.
7 Serve with fresh or stewed fruit.

Ukraine

Urban life in Ukraine has seen a trend towards modernisation in recent years. Western companies are making their arrival there and trendy European restaurants are shooting out of the ground like mushrooms. But in the country-side time seems virtually to have stood still. This is where tourists should go to find typical Ukrainian dishes, preferably as a guest in a Ukrainian household. That's where bortsch can be found simmering on the stove when the men come in from the fields: a nourishing concoction of beetroot, cabbage and meat that is a meal in itself. Ukrainians demonstrate their culinary skills mainly on festive occasions, when no dining table is complete without noodles, stuffed cabbage, hams, sausages, sweetened breads and cakes with fruit and honey. Between courses the guests let off steam with the hopak, the Ukrainian folk dance. Dancing and eating well into the small hours, with a glass of vodka at hand; that is probably the most delectable and pleasurable way to get to know Ukraine.

Scotch whisky trifle

TRIFLE:
500 g cake, cut into cubes
250 ml cream
100 ml whisky
4 tbs raspberry jam
1 punnet of raspberries
2 peeled bananas

FOR THE FILLING:
300 ml cream
150 ml milk
150 ml espresso coffee
1 vanilla pod, split
6 egg yolks
100 g demerara sugar
3 tbs flour
60 ml whisky

FOR THE TOPPING:
50 ml whisky
3 tbs sugar
a few raspberries
6 tbs chocolate,
chopped small

Filling:
1 Heat the milk and the vanilla pod with the coffee, and allow to stand for 20 minutes.
2 Remove the vanilla pod (leaving the inner pith).
3 Whisk the eggs with the cream and flour.
4 Add to the milk and bring to the boil, stirring until it begins to thicken.
5 Allow to cool and then stir in the whisky.

Trifle:
1 Arrange half of the cubes of cake in a bowl.
2 Sprinkle them with half of the whisky.
3 Whisk 250 mln cream to a soft peak and fold this into the filling.
4 Heat the jam.
5 Pour half of the warm jam on to the cake and pour half of the filling over it.
6 Arrange half of the raspberries and the banana on top.
7 Repeat these steps with the second half of the ingredients.
8 Allow the trifle to cool for 3 hours.
9 Decorate the trifle with raspberries and chopped chocolate.

United Kingdom

Five o'clock tea is the culinary high point of the day in the United Kingdom, most of all when guests are present. This is when the handmade porcelain china comes out of the cupboard, on which to serve the most delicious snacks. Sandwiches with smoked chicken and mayonnaise, scones with marmelade and fresh whipped cream, and sweets like the Scotch whisky trifle. British families keen to keep tradition alive pour their afternoon tea from a silver Victorian teapot with matching milk jug and sugar bowl. In good weather tea is served in the garden, on a well laid out terrace rimmed with flowers. The British are fond of spending their days off when weather permits on teatime picnic outings to parks or woodland. Picnics usually consist of an even bigger choice of delicacies, such as fresh salad, smoked salmon, chilled wine or champagne.

Arabian coffee with date cake

Qahwa ma'a tamar matbûkh

ARABIAN COFFEE:
¼ dl water
2 tsp sugar
(a modern habit)
2 ½ tsp dark roast coffee,
very finely ground
ground cardamom
orange flower water or
rosewater

DATE CAKE:
250 g dried stoned dates,
shredded
2 tbs sugar
2 tbs butter
50 g pistachio nuts,
chopped small
50 g flaked roast almonds
1 tbs sesame seed

1 Bring the required amount of water with the sugar to the boil in an Arabian coffee pot.
2 Take the water off the heat and add the coffee.
3 Bring it back to the boil.
4 When the foam rises to the surface, take the coffee off the heat and let the foam sink by tapping against the side of the pot.
5 Repeat these steps 3 times, but do not tap against the side of the pot the third time.
6 Pour into cups immediately and make sure everyone gets a bit of foam (this brings luck).
7 Add cardamom and orange flower water or rosewater to taste.

Date cake:
1 Simmer the dates, sugar and butter in a pan, stirring until the butter has been absorbed.
2 Add the nuts and sesame seed, stirring in well.
3 Take the mixture off the heat and pour it on to a lightly greased surface. Sprinkle with almond flakes.
4 Roll this out to a thickness of 1 ½ cm and slice into a diamond pattern.

United Arab Emirates

The population of the Emirates is highly variegated, with foreigners even forming a majority. Oil extraction, the industry that took off in the nineteen-sixties, has drawn workers from Asia, Europe and the United States. This trend has had its impact on the culinary culture of the Emirates, which is now typically international. The native population, nomadic since time immemorial, now prefer the foreign dishes that are available all over the region. But anyone who tries hard enough can still find traces of local traditions such as the coffee culture. The preparation of coffee, or qahwa, is a ceremonial procedure: the beans are first roasted before being crushed and mixed with cardamom. Coffee is poured out a little at a time, and guests drink it in tiny sips. If a guest shakes his cup from left to right it means he's had enough. The coffee is poured straight from the Arabian coffee pot or dallah. Served with date cake, qahwa forms the perfect finish to an evening lingering over a genuine Arabian repast.

Coconut cream

Coco quemado

500 ml milk
150 ml sweetened
coconut cream
12 egg yolks, loosely
whisked (or 7 eggs)
70 g cornflour
300 g sugar
150 g coconut, grated

1 Bring 350 ml milk to the boil with the coconut cream and the sugar and remove from the heat immediately.
2 Pour a little of the warm milk and coconut cream gradually on to the egg yolks, whisk it in and then return this to the pan with the remainder of the milk mixture.
3 Blend the cornflour into 150 ml milk and add this to the milk, coconut cream and eggs. Return the pan to the heat and whisk until it starts to thicken, then continue whisking until it has cooled off.
4 Toast the coconut and sprinkle over the coconut cream. Serve chilled.

Cuba

Cuba is the most westerly island of the Greater Antilles and also the largest of the Caribbean islands. In mediaeval times the Spaniards called it 'The key to the New World' because of its strategic position. Street life on the island is dynamic and cheerful. You can dance, sing and eat anywhere and everywhere whatever the time of day. While passersby eat their fill of Creole specialties at one of the many sidewalk stalls, bands and trova groups make their way through the street. Cuba's best-known products are its cigars and rum. But its exotic desserts are also not to be despised. This coco quemado brings the Caribbean atmosphere close to home.

Cherry fritters

Fritos de cerezas

1 egg yolk
80 ml milk
1 tbs butter, melted
100 g flour
icing sugar
2 egg whites
250 g cherries, stoned,
fresh or bottled
oil for deep–frying

1 Combine the egg yolk, milk and butter in a bowl.
2 Sieve the flour and sugar into another bowl, then mix in the egg mixture and whisk until soft.
3 Cover and allow to stand until ready to use.
4 Whisk the egg whites to a stiff peak and fold into the batter mixture.
5 Dry the cherries on a paper napkin.
6 Heat the oil, spike each cherry on to a kebab skewer and then dip each into the batter.
7 Fry the spiked cherries one by one in the oil until they are golden and crispy.
8 Allow to drain on a paper napkin and keep warm in the oven until all the cherry fritters have been fried.
9 Serve warm with ice cream and sprinkle with icing sugar.

Chile

In the ancient language of native Indians Chile means 'There where the land ends" – an appropriate name for this long strung out stretch of country edging South America between the Andes Mountains and the Pacific Ocean. The centre of Chile is a wide plain split by a fertile valley. The water in this region comes from small rivers draining the Andes. In this area many kinds of fruit and vegetables are cultivated, and are now increasingly being sold on export markets worldwide. Chilean wines also sell well on the international market. The viniculture industry came into being thanks to the Spaniards, who planted the country's first muscat grapes. Chilean growers later brought over French wine connoisseurs to cultivate French types of grape. As well as grapes, the main crops cultivated are apples, apricots, pears and cherries. The best cherries for cherry fritters come from central Chile. Fortunately these can often be found in our neighbourhood supermarkets.

Chocolate gateau

Sachertorte

FOR A GATEAU WITH A
DIAMETER OF
22 CENTIMETRES:
175 g bitter chocolate,
chopped or broken into
small pieces
8 egg yolks
110 g unsalted butter,
melted
1 tsp vanilla extract
10 egg whites
pinch of salt
120 g sugar
60 g flour
½ jar apricot jam

GLAZE:
85 g chocolate,
chopped or broken
into small pieces
100 ml cream

1 Line the base and sides of two round cake tins measuring 22 cm in diameter and 4 cm deep with greaseproof paper.
2 Melt the chocolate with the butter au bain marie (that is: in a small pan suspended in a larger pan containing hot water), stirring occasionally with a wooden spoon.
3 Whisk the egg yolks and sugar in a bowl until thick and stir in the chocolate butter and the vanilla extract.
4 Whisk the egg whites with a pinch of salt until they begin to foam, then add the sugar a spoonful at a time and continue whisking until they reach the stiff peak stage.
5 Fold about 1/3 of the whisked egg whites into the egg yolk and chocolate mixture, then reverse the process and fold the chocolate mixture into the rest of the egg white.
6 Sprinkle the flour on to the mixture. Fold flour, egg white and chocolate together until none of the egg white remains visible. Do not continue too long with this folding process.
7 Pour the mixture into the lined cake tins in two equal portions. Bake them in the oven at 170°C for about 35 minutes.
8 Melt chocolate and cream together in a small thick-bottomed pan. Allow this chocolate glaze to cool to room temperature.
9 When the two cakes are completely cool, spread one with apricot jam and place the other on top.
10 Place the rack with the cakes above a baking tray and tip the chocolate glaze from the pan on to the cakes from a height of 5 cm. Smooth it over, preferably with a spatula. Allow the cake to rest until the glaze has hardened and then transfer it, with the help of two knives, on to a plate.
11 Allow the glaze to harden and serve.

Austria

The culinary traditions of Austria stem from the era of the powerful Hapsburg empire, which also included present-day Hungary, the Czech Republic, Northern Italy and Istria. The Hapsburgers were fond of giving large dinner parties in their palaces. Famous composers like Mahler and Strauss were often welcome guests on such occasions. They shared in the enjoyment of the many delicacies arriving at the table on silver and gold serving dishes. The imperial traditions of olden times are still cherished in Austria. They survive in Vienna's stylish coffee houses, which still breathe the atmosphere of aristocratic life. Here, among the sumptuous cakes on display in polished glass showcases, you can find the Sachertorte, the most renowned of all Austrian confections. The first ever Sachertorte was made in 1832 by master baker Franz Sacher for Prince Klemens von Metternich. Sachertorte is still on the menu in Vienna's Sacher Hotel. It is always served with a glass of water to quench the thirst after all that sweetness.

REGISTER

WITH THANKS TO

The Embassy of Bahrain, Embassy of Brazil, Embassy of Bulgaria, Embassy of Canada, Embassy of Chile, Embassy of Colombia, Embassy of Ecuador, Embassy of Finland, Embassy of India, Embassy of Japan, Embassy of Malaysia, Embassy of Mexico, Embassy of Monaco, Embassy of Peru, Embassy of Poland, Embassy of Rumania, Embassy of the Slovak Republic, Embassy of Thailand, Embassy of Uruguay, Embassy of Zimbabwe (Brussels), Embassy of South Africa, Embassy of South Korea, the Australian Tourist Office, Chinese restaurant Hoo Wah, the Consulate of Paraguay, the Cuban Tourist Office, The Curaçao Tourist Office for Europe, The German Tourist Office, the French National Tourist Office, the Greek Tourist Office, the Indian Tourist Office, Royal Tropical Institute, the Korean Overseas Culture and Information Service, New Zealand Tourism Board, the Austrian Tourist Office, the Province of Limburg Tourism Department (Belgium), the Singapore Tourism Board, the Spanish Tourist Office, Tai Pei Representative Office, the Czech Bureau for Tourism, the Turkish Tourist Office, Switzerland Tourism, Abdul Bellari, Dorri te Boekhorst, Simone de Clerq, Jean Degen, Eiblin Fidder, Floor van der Gulik, Liselotte Hanff, Janou Hemsing, Amanda Kirk, Ben Klaassen, Shukri Omar Abdellahi, Qader Shafiq, Anita Timmermans, Peter Walch, Judy West, Marieke Wolf, Bonkers (Koziol), Clip BV, De Kaap N De Branding, and Wim Pollmann Sinds 1890.